CAO GUIMARÃES

LOCUS

JAAP GULDEMOND

MARENTE BLOEMHEUVEL

In an increasingly globalized world of shrinking distances, both literal and psychological, where we travel more but encounter more of the same, where the difference between one place and the next is narrowing – in this world, the work of Apichatpong Weerasethakul and Cao Guimarães stands out. Each of these artists explores in his work his immediate personal surroundings and what makes them unique. Theirs are oeuvres in which the locus, the place itself, plays a key role.

In biology, the word locus indicates the position of a gene on a chromosome. A list with the various positions (or loci) of the genes on a chromosome, an arrangement that ultimately determines the specific and unique character of the chromosome, is called a genetic map. One might draw an analogy and say that the work of Weerasethakul and Guimarães constitutes a genetic map of their immediate environment.

Both artists are deeply rooted in their respective local conditions. Apichatpong Weerasethakul is a Thai artist whose films, film installations, photos and experimental videos are set – with an occasional exception – in the north-east of Thailand, while the work of Cao Guimarães, born in Minas Gerais in Brazil, is very clearly embedded in his surroundings and in Brazilian culture.

Weerasethakul and Guimarães shift the focus away from the big narrative. What remains are moments in which they zoom in on seemingly unremarkable events, minor details of life elevated to a higher, more general level by the frame of Guimarães' camera. Or in the case of Weerasethakul, moments where life seems to pass by slowly and discreetly, but where plenty is happening beneath the surface. Apparently trivial events suddenly turn out to form part of a series of mysterious dream-images. Images appear and disappear in the blue-green dimness of the hallucinating jungle, which forms the perfect backdrop for his seamless transitions from reality to fiction and vice versa, the ideal setting for his reincarnations and transformations.

Cao Guimarães explores the lyric atmosphere of his surroundings in poetic imagery and saturated colours. There is often a certain domestic and prosaic feel to the settings – a small town with unpaved streets, where nature's presence is still felt for example, or a market where merchants sell their wares beneath canopies of coloured canvas.

Starting with the everyday life they see around them, these artists scrutinize their surroundings with an exceptionally keen eye that succeeds in revealing its beauty, colours, rhythms, details, sounds, shapes and scents. And that's not all. Beneath this layer of localness, their work engages with the narratives, history and socio-political situation of their country. The power of both their work lies for the most part in their ability to penetrate deeply into the locale and, at the same time, to imbue it with universal relevance.

Each of these oeuvres contains imagery from a different part of the world, expressing the individual, specific character of a particular place. Imagery that runs counter to a globalist world view, to the process of economic, political and cultural integration in which everything starts to look the same. Both Apichatpong and Guimarães turn their gaze on their immediate surroundings, immersing their work in their locality, in the town where they live, the people who live there, the nature around them. That is why their film works express a physical proximity, while issues of a wider cultural or political nature are more implicit, 'beyond the frame'. The local environment not only forms a backdrop but also carries meanings and connotations shaped by the history of the place and its people. In the work of Guimarães, for example, we encounter references to an old folk healer, to the popular game of bocce (a variant of boules), and to the important Brazilian traditions of carnival and Ash Wednesday (the day after carnival). In addition to making frequent, indirect references to the complex political situation in Thailand, Weerasethakul enriches his magical films with local myths, fables and folklore.

CAO GUIMARÃES

Cao Guimarães was born in 1965 in Belo Horizonte, Brazil. He studied philosophy and photography, and since the early 1990s he has made numerous short films, photographic works and nine feature films and long documentaries. His work is situated at the interface between cinema and visual art. The films have been screened at major film festivals around the world, including Locarno, Cannes, Rotterdam, Sundance and Venice. It has also been exhibited and purchased by leading museums such as the Guggenheim Museum in New York, Museu Inhotim in Belo Horizonte, Museo Jumex in Mexico City, Fondation Cartier in Paris and Tate Modern in London.

Just like Apichatpong Weerasethakul, Guimarães has a remarkable eye for minor occurrences, objects, colours and sounds that normally escape people's attention. He shows commonplace events in his immediate surroundings in such a way that the 'ordinary' becomes extraordinary, yet not detached from everyday experience. Guimarães' power lies in discovering an unexpected magic in the mundane. In both the literal and the figurative senses, he is more interested in so-called micro-events than in macro-events. His films are populated by minuscule insects, soap bubbles, raindrops, petals falling on the ground, 'gambiarras' (small 'discoveries' that allow life to proceed), footprints and fluffy seeds floating in the air. Moreover, Guimarães is drawn to precisely those places where people live but are often overlooked, people who avoid the predictably structured lives we are expected to live in modern capitalist society. Not only the drifters, homeless and hermits on the fringes of society, but also children who to him represent the freedom to live as you want, devoid
of rules of conduct and full of uncertainty about how to proceed. Guimarães presents us with alternative ways of living, inviting us to break free from our own structured lives.

Other important elements in his work are the landscape and natural phenomena like sunlight, weather, or reflections of light on water. What is striking is that the relationship between people and their natural environment is not a hierarchical one but a seamless connection. As already noted, the work of Guimarães is situated at the interface between cinema and art. Self-taught, he pays little heed to prevailing conventions and predictable forms of filmmaking. He films in a seemingly intuitive manner, with a keen eye for detail and colour. Although documentary by nature, his images seem to float between familiar reality and a world in which the senses take precedence and – as in the work of Weerasethakul – free themselves from rational considerations. In that way, Guimarães' imagery evokes a world that blends dream, sensual experience and reality. Slow camera movements, long lingering shots, an often striking texture, but above all a strong sense of colour and composition – all this ensures that Guimarães' work deepens into a perceptive phenomenology.

Delicately appealing to the senses, Guimarães' short films are small, self-contained worlds that zoom in on one element, for example on the wonderfully time-worn hands of an old black Brazilian folk healer, or a pair of kites swirling playfully against a blue sky, or the light reflected in a soap bubble drifting through the air, or the colourful clocks, filmed head on, used for keeping score during a game of bocce. Another film shows Guimarães' awareness and keen eye for the beauty of the mundane. In the film **Limbo** we see forlorn playground equipment, without children, as a study of forms. The swings, roundabout and other objects are still moving slightly, as though just abandoned. In **Quarta-feira de cinzas (Epilogue: Ash Wednesday**, 2006) Guimarães conveys the subtle relationship between humankind and nature by showing how, on Ash Wednesday, the day after carnival, industrious ants carry strewn confetti back to their nest one piece at a time.

Guimarães' high-spirited dedication to the life around him is matched by a similar dedication to people and events. He records this life like a cartographer, in the process revealing his attraction to those places where 'informal' life plays out. Or as a Brazilian critic recently wrote: 'His work translates as a resistance strategy against the utilitarian comprehension of the world, discarding or despising everything that does not obey its logic.'[1]

1 Moacir dos Anjos, Cao Guimarães, **Cao**, São Paulo, Cosac Naify, 2015, p. 261.

A FABLE

CONSUELO LINS

SEEING IS

Extracting poetry from any reality, glimpsing the virtually poetic in ordinary shapes from life and nature: these are central traits of Cao Guimarães' work method. That is, if we can call a 'method' the Brazilian artist's intuitive skill in recording what unveils itself before his eyes and his receptiveness to the textures and temporalities of the world's sensory events. If there is a method, it is expressed in the gesture of framing and composing what he sees, often right next to him in his life's most domestic sphere, and in deriving artistic power from apparently unimportant beings, things and situations: children playing in the rain in **Da janela do meu quarto (From the Window of My Room)**, a street fair's coloured awnings in **Sin peso (Weightless)**, ants carrying Mardi Gras confetti in **Quarta-feira de cinzas (Epilogue: Ash Wednesday)**, veils of all kinds scattered around the city in **O sonho da casa própria (Veiled Dream)**, or a black woman's praying hands in **Reza (Prayer)**. The artist plastically investigates aspects of everyday life by creating micronarratives or 'quasi-narratives', often ephemeral sensory configurations on the verge of disappearing. Meanwhile, he dissolves the utilitarian order that constrains everyday things within a certain kind of logic and releases them for other sensory existences. 'I would rather pursue sensations than the logical sense of things,' says Cao Guimarães.[1]

Perhaps the ability to see poetry everywhere relates somehow to the time he spent in his childhood on a farm in the hinterlands of Minas Gerais, living with his grandfather, a paediatrician, photographer and amateur filmmaker. His apprenticeship in daily observations of ants, spiders and other insects and creatures, his contemplation of the world, and the exercise of slow and idle time all may have honed the artist's senses for hovering attentively over the world's sensory facts, and later in life, drawing on all this as raw material for his creative works. 'I have a PhD in ants,' says Manoel de Barros in a poem,[2] a claim Cao Guimarães could also make as an expert in insects and a microscopic world nearly invisible to the naked eye, often recorded with equipment passed down from his grandfather. 'I inherited more from my grandfather than just his Super8 camera, 16mm spring-wound Bolex, 35mm Nikon, and photo laboratory. I inherited his love for the image.'

Regardless of how the artist's predisposition emerged and matured, we find 'artistic material' made of sensory experiences in most of his works, whether photographs, installations, writings or shorts and feature films, produced regularly since the early 2000s. While we identify this 'material' more easily in Cao's shorter works, it also appears in his other projects produced in different media and in various time frames. In his documentaries, he aims his camera at anonymous individuals, and what interests him is also their sensory experience with everything that surrounds them. The hermit Dominguinhos da Pedra in **A alma do osso (The Soul of the Bone**, 2004) is less a character than a 'being of sensations' ready to capture the intensities of the sun, the wind, the earth, the hills, to focus on nature's microscopic nature and the sensory events around him.

BETWEEN ART AND FILM

The constant presence of the artist's works in both art and cinema in the last fifteen years makes him the most successful Brazilian artist working in these two artistic territories, with his work exhibited in galleries, museums and cultural institutions and as part of prestigious collections, besides having been selected for (and won) awards at major international film festivals. His most celebrated short film, **Da janela do meu quarto** (2004), is a prime example of this fluid circulation between cinema and art: it premiered at the Cannes Film Festival and was subsequently screened at art events around the world. The documentary **Andarilho (Drifter)** opened the 27th São Paulo Biennial in 2007 and was screened at international film festivals (Venice, Rotterdam, Locarno) and distributed commercially in movie theatres in Brazil.

Cao Guimarães became a movie lover when he was still an undergraduate philosophy student, attracted by films that 'sculpt time', to quote his favourite filmmaker, Andrei Tarkosvky. He admired Michelangelo Antonioni, the New German Cinema, Nouvelle Vague and Werner Herzog. But it was virtually impossible to make films in Belo Horizonte in the late 1980s. Photography and writing were feasible alternatives that gave him the independence that cinema was apparently unable to provide at the time.

His contact with friends in the various fine arts opened possibilities for a more hybrid creative path. Propositional artistic experiments with a conceptual dimension attracted his attention: work whose point of departure was the artists' own definition of the rules, subsequently unfolding in sensory investigations. Cao organized his first such experiment in the mid-1990s. In **Histórias do não ver (Stories of Not Seeing)**, in which he arranged to be kidnapped and blindfolded by friends in order to experience situations through other senses than sight. This proposition allowed the artist to strip himself of his visual impressions, of the logic and habits proper to sight: 'I wanted to feel the world only through what I was hearing, smelling, touching, thinking. Sight had always seemed tyrannical to me when compared to the other senses. Without sight, the world could thus become several worlds, and one reality could become several realities.'[3]

Cinema became a real possibility while Cao was living in London (1996–1998) with artist Rivane Neuenschwander. He decided to use his grandfather's Super8 to record his daily comings and goings in this previously unfamiliar city, and perhaps for that very reason he was more alert to his perceptions and sensations, even the most fleeting, at home, on the streets, and in the parks where he took walks. This footage formed a film file that fascinated him, and he referred to this 'little exercise of solitary observation of the world' as his 'kitchen cinema', 'cinema that comes from indoors, from the afternoon light shining on the tiles, the bean that falls from the colander, full of presence and life'.[4] These images served as the basis for his first short films, **The Eye Land** (1999) and **Between – Inventário de pequenas mortes (Between – An Inventory of Minor Deaths**, 2000). The London experience was decisive for modulating an aesthetic stance open to the poetry hidden in every sensory reality.

It was as if he realized that sight was not necessarily a 'tyrannical sense'. Rather, it was necessary to liberate sight, and the body, from a tyranny that prevented him from perceiving 'the expressiveness of the minimum', 'the simplicity of things, and not this whole lot of adjectives and layers placed on photographs to make them aesthetic'. It was necessary 'to view the world and phenomena in their simplicity, in their essence, to strip reality of adjectives to seek its substantiality'.[5] He thus realized that the moving image could enter the universe of art in singular practices, detached from expensive productions, yet without failing to reclaim a certain spirit of filmmaking experimentation.

While most of Cao Guimarães' photographs and short films resulted from casual filming, his propositional gesture appears in some projects, especially partnerships with Rivane Neuenschwander. Still, these projects are more subtle performative acts such as producing soap bubbles on the landscape for the short film **Sopro (Blow**, 2000) or minimal acts with ants as characters, as in **Word/World** (2001) and **Quarta-feira de cinzas** (2006). In such playful experiments, reminiscent of children's games, the artist performs little interventions to better observe sensorial changes in the landscape. His experiments with ants disrupt their utilitarian logic by introducing words (word and world) on slips of paper in an anthill, which looks more like a forced labour camp, or by scattering coloured confetti that brightens these tiny creatures marching to and fro. The title, **Quarta-feira de cinzas**, refers to the end of Mardi Gras, the end of the party, the after everything, except for the ants that labour to cart away the confetti strewn on the ground.

The anthill's sounds in **Quarta-feira de cinzas** gradually take on the rhythm of Mardi Gras drumming in a soundtrack recorded by O Grivo, in which the musicality emerges from the way the sounds of the ants in action are reconfigured. Nelson Soares and Marcos Moreira have been Cao Guimarães' partners since his early projects, and the musical duet's sonorous poetics are essential to the sensory impact of the artist's shorts and feature films. 'With O Grivo (and John Cage via O Grivo), I learned to listen (…) I learned to respect and take special care of each particle of sound our

ears capture, including the ones we imagine.'
The soundtracks by O Grivo distil pieces of
conversations, fragments of songs, murmurs,
noises, silences, associating them with sounds
generated by the most outlandish objects. They
polish an infinite range of sounds that gain unprecedented clarity to our ears (the drumming
of raindrops in **Da janela do meu quarto**), an
unexpected musicality (street vendors' voices in
Sin peso), and micronarratives (commentary and
conversation in **Jogo** (**Game**)). We can be surpri-
sed by the expressive force of sonorities that
are familiar, but that we tend to ignore in everyday life. This poetic trait in crafting the sounds
echoes with Cao Guimarães' construction of
his images, activating poetry in things that go
unnoticed in daily routine.

Cao Guimarães expanded his taste for a
cinema that 'sculpts time' in his documentaries
from the early 2000s. Having no previous contact with this form of cinema, Cao made his first
such film the same way he invented 'kitchen cinema': engaging directly with the practice, moved
by the desire to make unfamiliar things. By filming
professions on the verge of extinction in **O fim do
sem fim** (**The End of the Endless**, 2001), the pas-
sage of time in backwater towns in Minas Gerais
in **Acidente** (**Accident**), a hermit in **A alma do
osso** (**The Soul of the Bone**, 2004), and vaga-
bonds in **Andarilho** (**Drifter**, 2007), the artist
shifts 'outside of himself' to real situations, land-
scapes and individuals, drawing him closer to
documentary, even unintentionally. The relationship with 'the other', so central to documentary
tradition, took roads less travelled. The filmmaker
took an interest in solitary characters with obscure
existences on the fringes of social dynamics, of
the formal economy, and of productivist logic,
meanwhile surviving on the ability to create sub-
sistence out of very little. Precisely because he
was a foreigner in the land of documentary and
his formal investigations were more contained
in these films, the narratives minimalist, and the
temporality extended, his unprecedented attention to the insignificant and to the tininess of ordinary environments ended up influencing novice
Brazilian documentarians in the early 2000s.

CHILDHOOD AND POETRY

In **Da janela do meu quarto**, two children are
playing at fighting in the rain, soaked and bare-
foot in the mud. The boy is wearing blue bathing
trunks, and the girl is wearing red shorts and has
her hair in pigtails. The reflections of their bodies
paint a dance in the puddles, switching roles back
and forth. The girl has the stubborn courage of
one who doesn't calculate the risks, but trusts in
her adversary's clemency. She lurches fearlessly
at the boy, making circular movements with her
arms in a graceful choreography repeated over
and over in the game.

This short film exudes children's ability to de-
rive pleasure from so little, their inclination to acti-
vate their own sensitivity to enjoy the experience
of being entirely in the game's here-and-now, with
no before and no after. While children do inhabit
some of Cao Guimarães' projects, fundamental
childhood traits permeate nearly all of the artist's
work with power, even his many videos and films
in which we see elderly characters, as in **Reza** and
Jogo. Childhood emerges in the way Cao affirms
intuition and sensitivity as modes of perceiving
and being affected by the world, of experiencing
the 'time of now' so dear to Walter Benjamin, of
feeling the materiality of things in a way that time-
hardened adults are no longer able. As Manoel de
Barros reminds us, 'Poetry plays the role of preaching
the practice of childhood among men.'[6] Thus, for
the poet and the artist, childhood is neither a lost
experience from a faraway past nor merely a chro-
nological moment in individuals' lives. Childhood
is a human dimension that echoes in the present
and emerges as a creative gesture in all our lives.

'Seeing is a fable' appropriately defines the
underlying aesthetic stance in many of Cao Guimarães' works. Quoted from Paulo Leminski's
Catatau (the novel that inspired Cao to make his
first fiction film, **Ex Isto** (**Ex It**), in 2010), the phrase
was chosen as the title for an important retrospec-
tive exhibition. In a sense, children see the world
'as a fable', through their enchantment with the
most mundane things in life, their curiosity towards ants and soap bubbles. 'Seeing is a fable'
means looking at the coloured awnings in a street
market in Mexico City (**Sin peso**, 2007) and seeing

varied monochromatic compositions – blue, pink, orange, green, living colours in movement – and also glimpsing, at the intersection of these awnings, geometric shapes with multiple textures, shades and modulations. 'Seeing is a fable' means creating planes that transform space through rigorous framing that joins patches of awning to fragments of sky. 'Seeing is a fable' means drawing unusual analogies between bridal veils and safety mesh screens on building constructions and producing micronarratives between sounds and images in **O sonho da casa própria** (2008). It means composing planes that evoke a pictorial imagery akin to geometric abstraction from the most ordinary reality.

Likewise, we are awed by the hands of the old folk healer in **Reza** (2016), with her long fingers making graceful gestures; fingers full of colourful rings that intermingle with the colours of the little woollen cardigan, the cloth bracelet, and the surviving flecks of her fingernail polish. It means letting ourselves be swept away by this stately woman at the pinnacle of her decades of experience, whispering prayers to ward off evil eyes and to undo spells, blessing the artist for whatever comes his way: 'You are ready, sir,' she says at the end. Her rosary of heavy glass beads, crucifix in the midst of necklaces, and a profusion of colours and materials evokes a traditional Brazilian religion blending Catholicism, indigenous culture, and African rituals. 'Seeing is a fable' is letting ourselves be permeated by what enraptures us. It is seeing more, surrendering to the fabulous dimension of sight and the other senses.

What do old folks and children share in Cao's work? What do an elderly healer woman, pensioners playing bocce, children dancing in the rain, a hermit and drifters have in common? They are characters living in a different time, outside the rat race, who no longer respond to the demands of work, meanwhile surviving on their ability to invent a life, fables, or games from this near nothing. This ability in children is more intuitive and auspicious, but in the elderly it can also mean an intense link to the present, whether retreating to the mountains, drifting apart from the world on the back roads of Minas Gerais, praying, or playing.

Jogo conducts a visual materialization of a burlesque version of a time unhinged, a time of playfulness and games: in the video we see two coloured clocks, each with just one hand. The clocks are not keeping time, but the score in the bocce game. To the right of these two scorekeepers and slightly in the background, a yardstick dangles, swaying like a pendulum. It is an audio-visual formulation reminiscent of a decomposed clock, a mad hatter's pocket watch where keeping time is irrelevant, while the clock's hands are moved by hand, at the players' whim. Not that there are no rules, but here the rules are internal to the game and negotiated by the players themselves. The soundtrack (O Grivo) is made up of snatches of conversation, interjections, murmurs, brief remarks, someone dialling a telephone, balls bouncing, and an occasional trombone. As if these clocks have rebelled against the tyranny of a quantitative and homogeneous time, always equal to itself, in favour of a more intense and dense time, full of presences.

In the face of the 'sensory objects' made by Cao Guimarães, viewers are invited to open their senses to the world. These objects are images and sounds that sensitize us to a sensorial dimension of the quotidian, plucking us out of our inertia, out of our ordinary, utilitarian attitude towards life. Gazing at the sky and seeing an infinite array of poetic possibilities, peering at the ground and identifying a myriad of sensorial events, glancing next to us and seeing a formal exuberance, a profusion of beings, colours, textures – 'transitory splendours', as Virginia Woolf would say, reminding us that 'beauty is everywhere'[7] and that everything is proper material for art.

1   Quotes by Cao Guimarães without footnotes are taken
    from the author's conversations with the artist.
2   Manoel de Barros, **Poesia Completa**. São Paulo: Texto
    Editora, 2010, p.392.
3   Cao Guimarães, in the introduction to the book **Histórias
    do não ver**. Rio de Janeiro: Cobogó, 2013, p.11.
4   Cao Guimarães in 'Cinema de cozinha' (Kitchen Cinema),
    written by the artist for the retrospective exhibition of the
    same name at SESC in São Paulo in 2008.
5   Cao Guimarães interviewed by Carla Zaccagnini by email
    for the 2nd San Juan Poly/Graphic Triennial (2009).
6   Manoel de Barros, **Gramática Expositiva do Chão:
    Poesia quase toda**. Rio de Janeiro: 1992,
    Civilização Brasileira, p.311.
7   Virginia Woolf, 'How it strikes a Contemporary'
    and 'Montaigne' in **The Common Reader**, A Project
    Gutenberg of Australia eBook, 2003, pp.131 and 43.

Consuelo Lins is an essayist, researcher and full professor
at Universidade Federal do Rio de Janeiro, Brazil. She holds
a PhD in cinema and audio-visual arts from the Université
de Paris (1994) and a post-doctoral degree from Birkbeck,
University of London (2015). She is the author of, among
others, **The documentary work of Eduardo Coutinho:
film, television, and video** (O documentário de Eduardo
Coutinho: cinema, televisão e vídeo, 2004) and co-author
with Cláudia Mesquita, of **Filming the real: on contemporary Brazilian documentary** (Filmar o real: sobre o
documentário brasileiro contemporâneo, 2011).

BIOGRAPHY & WORKS

CAO GUIMARÃES

BIOGRAPHY
WORKS
CAO GUIMARÃES

SIN PESO (WEIGHTLESS) 2007
Single-channel video installation
Super8 on DV, colour, 7'
Sound: O Grivo

**DA JANELA DO MEU QUARTO
(FROM THE WINDOW OF MY ROOM)** 2004
Single-channel video installation
Super8 on 35mm, colour, 5'
Sound: O Grivo

JOGO (GAME) 2016
Single-channel video installation
HD video, colour, 5'
Sound: O Grivo

REZA (PRAYER) 2016
Single-channel video installation
HD video, colour, 4'
Sound: O Grivo

O SONHO DA CASA PRÓPRIA (VEILED DREAM) 2008
Single-channel video installation
HD video, colour, 15'
Sound: O Grivo (multi-channel, 5.1)

Cao Guimarães & Rivane Neuenschwander
**QUARTA-FEIRA DE CINZAS
(EPILOGUE: ASH WEDNESDAY)** 2006
Single-channel video installation
HD video, colour, 6' Sound: O Grivo

Cao Guimarães & Rivane Neuenschwander
SOPRO (BLOW) 2000
Single-channel video installation
Super8 on DV, b&w, 5'30''
No sound

HYPNOSIS 2001
Single-channel video installation
Super8 on DV, colour, 7'30''
Sound: O Grivo

Cao Guimarães & Rivane Neuenschwander
WORD/WORLD 2001
Single-channel video installation
Super8 on DV, b&w, 7'
Sound: O Grivo

Cao Guimarães & Rivane Neuenschwander
**O INQUILINO
(THE TENANT)** 2010
Single-channel video installation
HD video, colour, 11'
Sound: O Grivo

LIMBO 2011
Single-channel video installation
HD video, colour, 17'
Sound: O Grivo

**A ALMA DO OSSO
(THE SOUL OF THE BONE)** 2004
Feature film
Super8 and DV, colour, 74'
Sound: O Grivo

OTTO 2012
Feature film
HD video, colour, 71'
Sound: O Grivo

All images © and courtesy Cao Guimarães

Cao Guimarães (b. 1965, Belo Horizonte, Brazil) lives and works in Belo Horizonte and in Montevideo, Uruguay. Considered one of Brazil's most prolific contemporary artists, Guimarães works at the intersection of visual art and cinema. Although known for his short films and video installations, he has also been making feature films, documentaries and photographic works since the late 1980s. His work has been collected by various prestigious museums including Tate Modern in London, MoMA and Guggenheim Museum in New York, Fondation Cartier in Paris, Colección Jumex in Mexico City, Museu Inhotim in Belo Horizonte and Museo Thyssen-Bornemisza in Madrid.

He has participated in many major exhibitions and events, including the 25th and 27th São Paulo Biennial; inSITE, Tijuana; Cruzamentos: Contemporary Art in Brazil, Columbus (Ohio); Tropicália: The 60s in Brazil, Vienna; Sharjah Biennial 11 Film Programme; and Ver é Uma Fábula, a large mid-career survey featuring most of the artist's works at Itaú Cultural, São Paulo. He is the director of nine feature films: Homen das multidões (The Man of the Crowd, 2013), Otto (2012), Elvira Lorelay – Alma de Dragón (2012), Ex-Isto (Ex It, 2010), Andarilho (Drifter, 2007), Acidente (Accident, 2006), A alma do osso (The Soul of the Bone, 2004), Rua de mão dupla (Two Way Street, 2002), and O fim do sem fim (The End of the Endless, 2001). His latest film, Waiting (provisional title), is set for release in 2017. Cao Guimarães has screened his films at major international film festivals, including Cannes, Locarno, Sundance, Venice, Rotterdam and Berlin. His films have been the subject of retrospectives at MoMA in New York (2011), the Buenos Aires International Festival of Independent Cinema (2014) and National Cinematheque in Mexico City (2014).

MONOGRAPHS

Cao Guimarães, Moacir dos Anjos
Cao, São Paulo, Cosac Naify, 2015

Ricardo Sardenberg (Ed.)
Cao Guimarães
Centro de Arte de Burgos, 2007

Cao Guimarães,
Teodoro Rennó Assunção
Histórias do não ver
published by Cao Guimarães, 2001

CREDITS

This book was published
on the occasion of the exhibition
Locus: Apichatpong Weerasethakul – Cao Guimarães,
EYE Filmmuseum, Amsterdam
16 September – 3 December, 2017

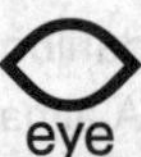

IJpromenade 1031 KT Amsterdam,
the Netherlands +31 (0) 20 5891400
info@eyefilm.nl

EXHIBITION

The exhibition was curated by Jaap Guldemond
in collaboration with Marente Bloemheuvel

CEO EYE **Sandra den Hamer**
Director of Exhibitions | Curator **Jaap Guldemond**
Associate Curator **Marente Bloemheuvel**
Project Managers **Sanne Baar, Claartje Opdam**
Graphic Design **Joseph Plateau, Amsterdam**
Film Programmer **Dana Linssen**
Publicity and Marketing **Inge Scheijde, Marnix van Wijk**
Technical Production **Rembrandt Boswijk, Indyvideo,
    Utrecht, and Bo Jansen**
Subtitling **Haghefilm Digitaal, Amsterdam**
Audiovisual Equipment **Eidotech, Berlin**
Installation **Syb Sybesma, Landstra & De Vries,
    Amsterdam**
Lighting **Maarten Warmerdam,
    Theatermachine, Amsterdam**

PUBLICATION

Edited by **Marente Bloemheuvel, Jaap Guldemond**
Essays **Consuelo Lins, Dana Linssen**
Graphic Design **Irma Boom Office, Amsterdam
    Irma Boom** and **Odilon Coutarel**
Translations **Billy Nolan (Dutch–English),
    Christopher Peterson (Portuguese–English)**
Copy Editing **Marente Bloemheuvel, Billy Nolan**
Proof reading **Robyn Dalziel**
Project Managers **Sanne Baar, Claartje Opdam**
Printing and lithography **Lenoirschuring, Amsterdam**
Paper **IBO One, 60gsm, IGEPA**
Font **Neuzit S IB**
Publisher **EYE Filmmuseum, Amsterdam
    nai010 publishers, Rotterdam**

ACKNOWLEDGEMENTS

Cao Guimarães
Apichatpong Weerasethakul
and **Studio Cao Guimarães,**
    Ralph Antunes, Belo Horizonte
    Kick the Machine Films, Bangkok
    Sompot Chidgasornpongse
    Simon Field
    Consuelo Lins
    Dana Linssen
    Volksbühne Berlin
    Österreichisches Filmmuseum, Vienna

IMAGES

All images © and courtesy Cao Guimarães

© 2017 Cao Guimaraes, the authors,
the photographers, EYE Filmmuseum Amsterdam,
nai010 publishers, Rotterdam

The exhibition and this publication were made possible
with the financial support of:

BankGiroLoterij   **FONDS 21**   AOM / DOM

All rights reserved. No part of this publication may be
reproduced, stored in a retrieval system, or transmitted
in any form or by any means, electronic, mechanical,
photocopying, recording or otherwise, without the
prior written permission of the publisher.

Every effort has been made to obtain the necessary
permissions to reproduce all copyrighted material
contained in this book. Should copyright have been
unwittingly infringed in this book, interested parties are
requested to contact nai010 publishers, Mauritsweg 23,
3012 JR Rotterdam, the Netherlands, info@nai010.com

nai010 publishers is an internationally orientated
publisher specialized in developing, producing
and distributing books on architecture, visual arts
and related disciplines. www.nai010.com

nai010 books are available internationally at selected
bookstores and from the following distribution
partners: North, Central and South America –
Artbook D.A.P., New York, USA, dap@dapinc.com

Rest of the world – Idea Books, Amsterdam,
the Netherlands, idea@ideabooks.nl
For general questions, please contact nai010
publishers directly at sales@nai010.com or visit
our website www.nai010.com for further information.

Printed and bound in the Netherlands
ISBN 978-94-6208-416-2

WEBSITE

caoguimaraes.com

GALLERIES

Galerie Nara Roesler
São Paulo | Rio de Janeiro | New York
Xippas Galerie, Paris | Montevideo

NAI010 PUBLISHERS
EYE FILMMUSEUM

THE WORK FROM THE WINDOW OF MY ROOM

CAO GUIMARÃES

SIN PESO (WEIGHTLESS)

2007

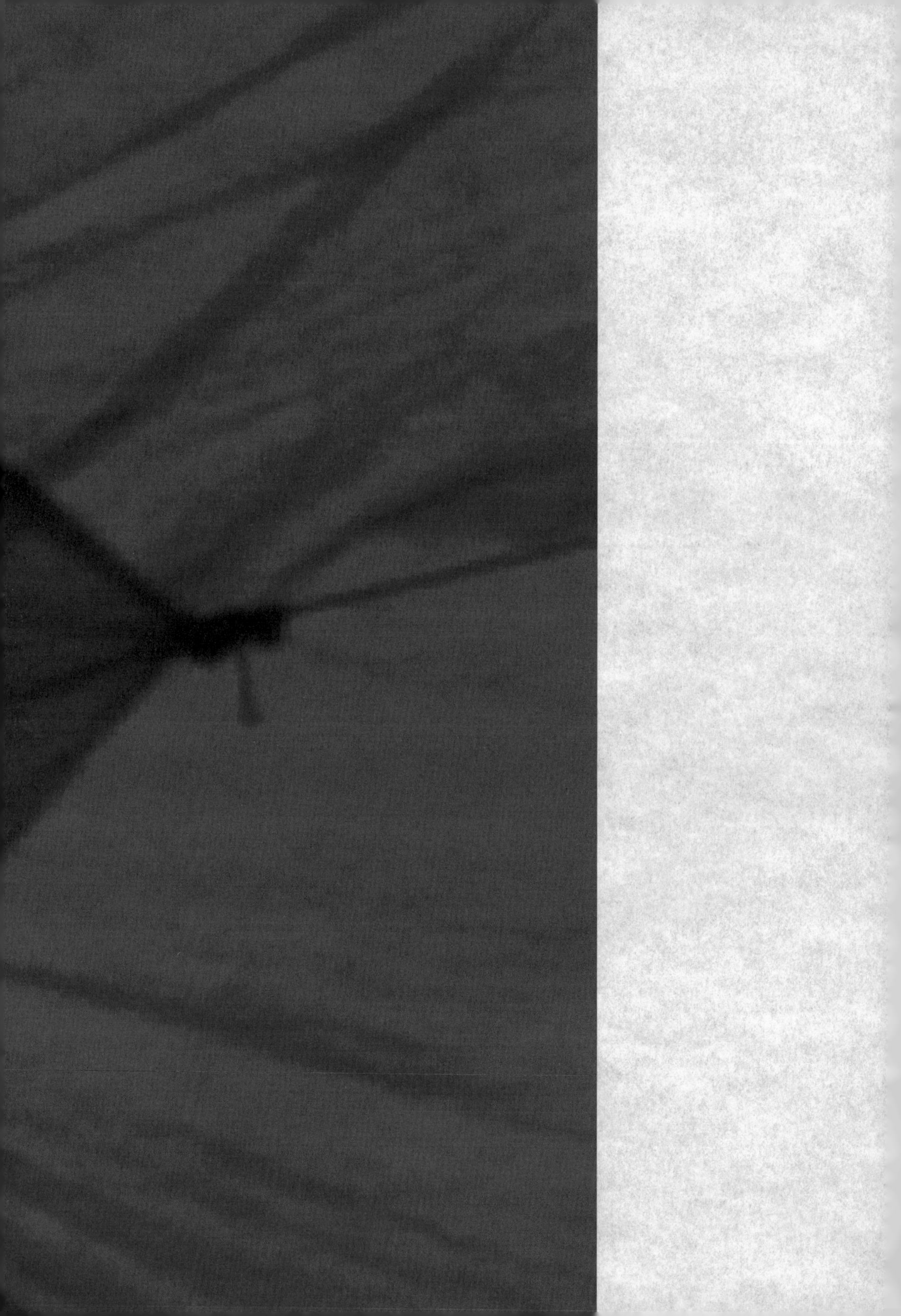

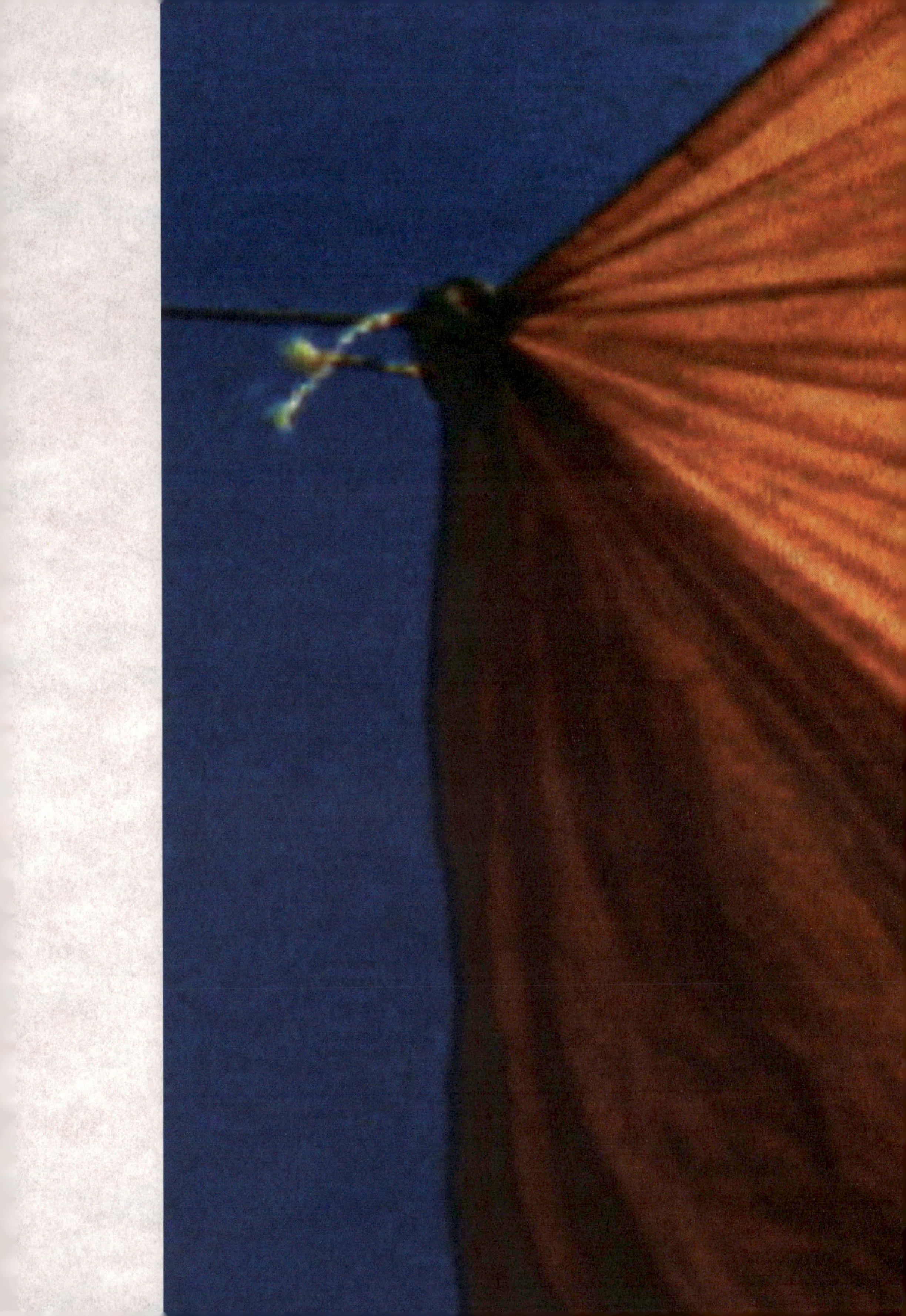

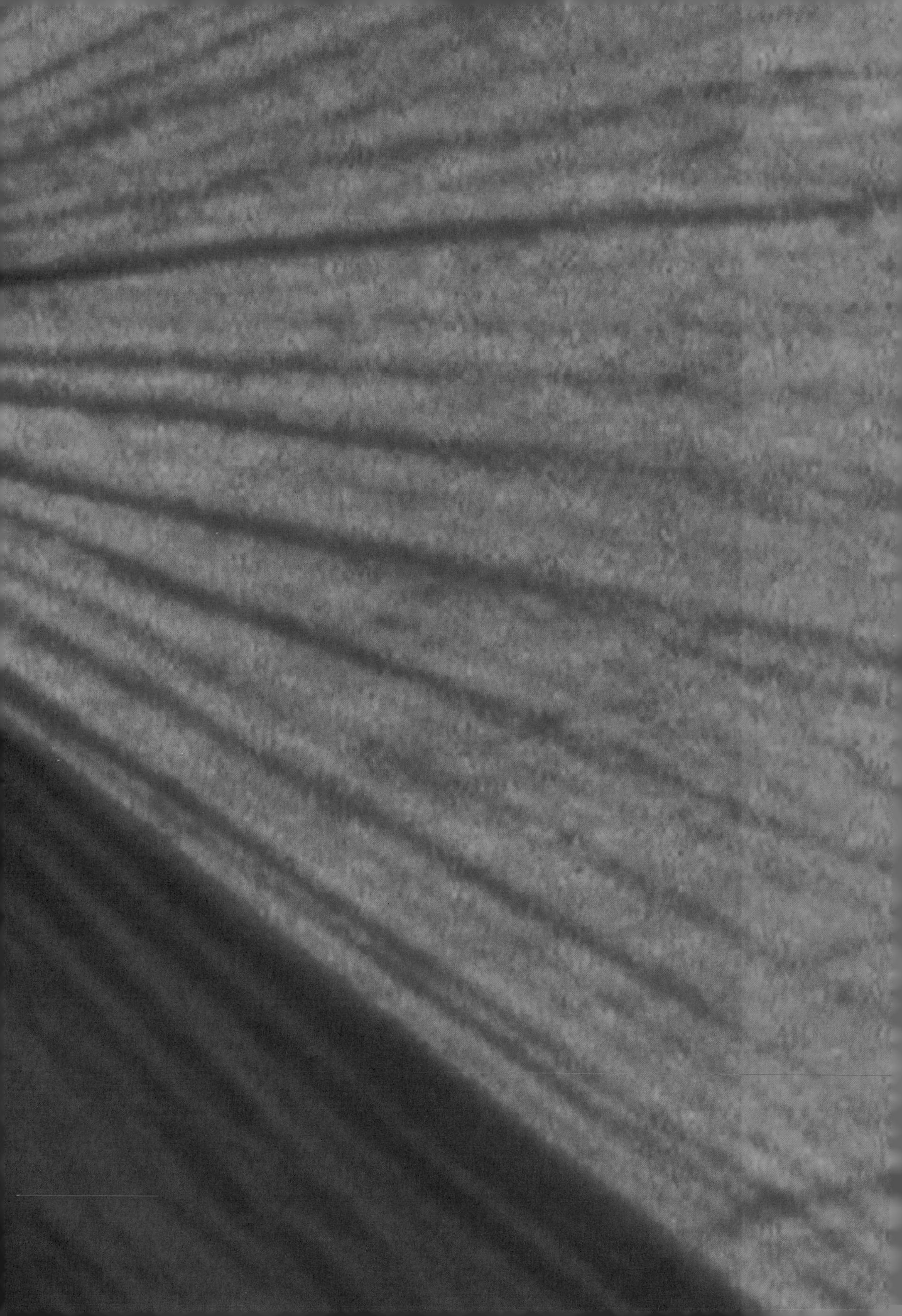

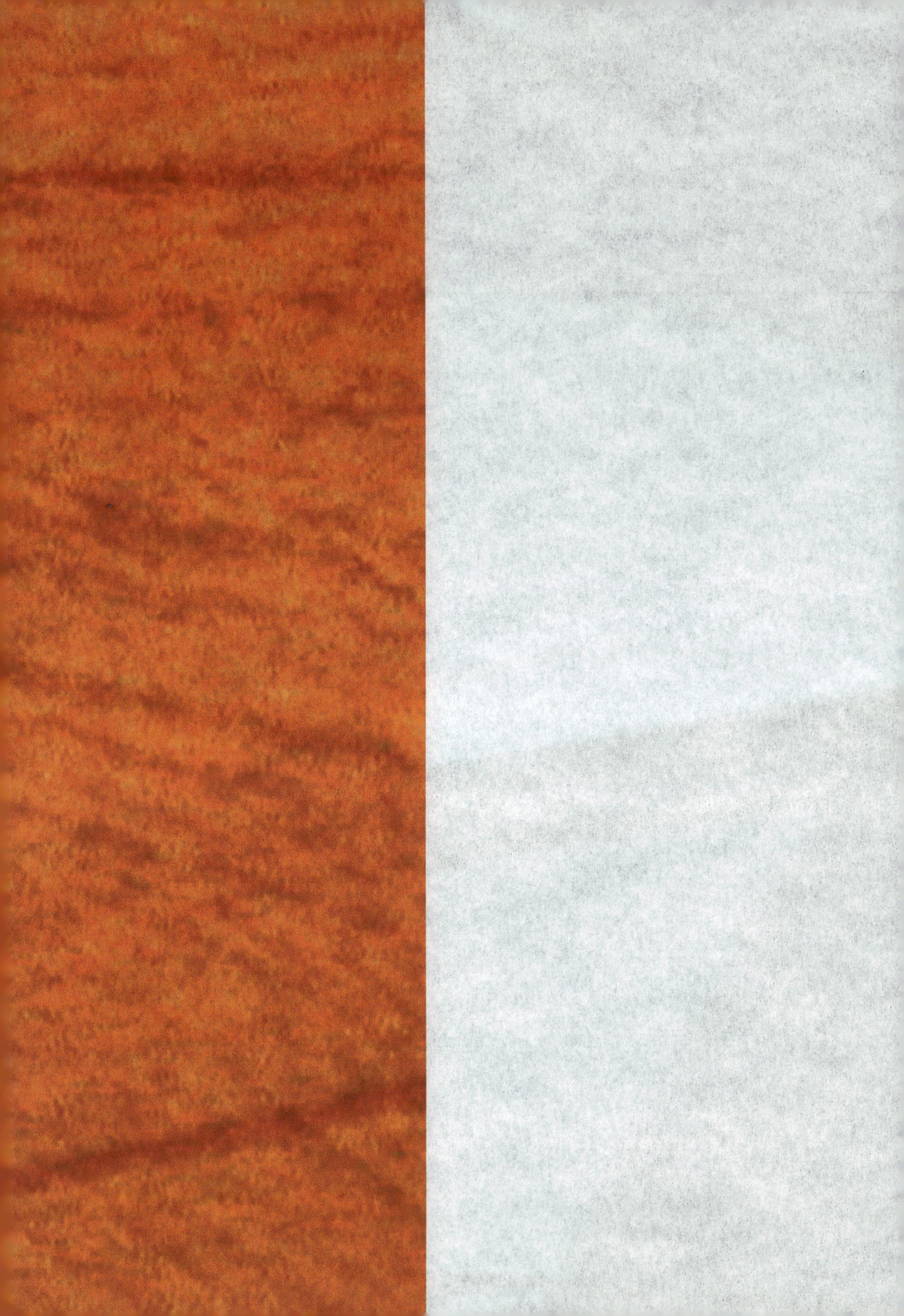

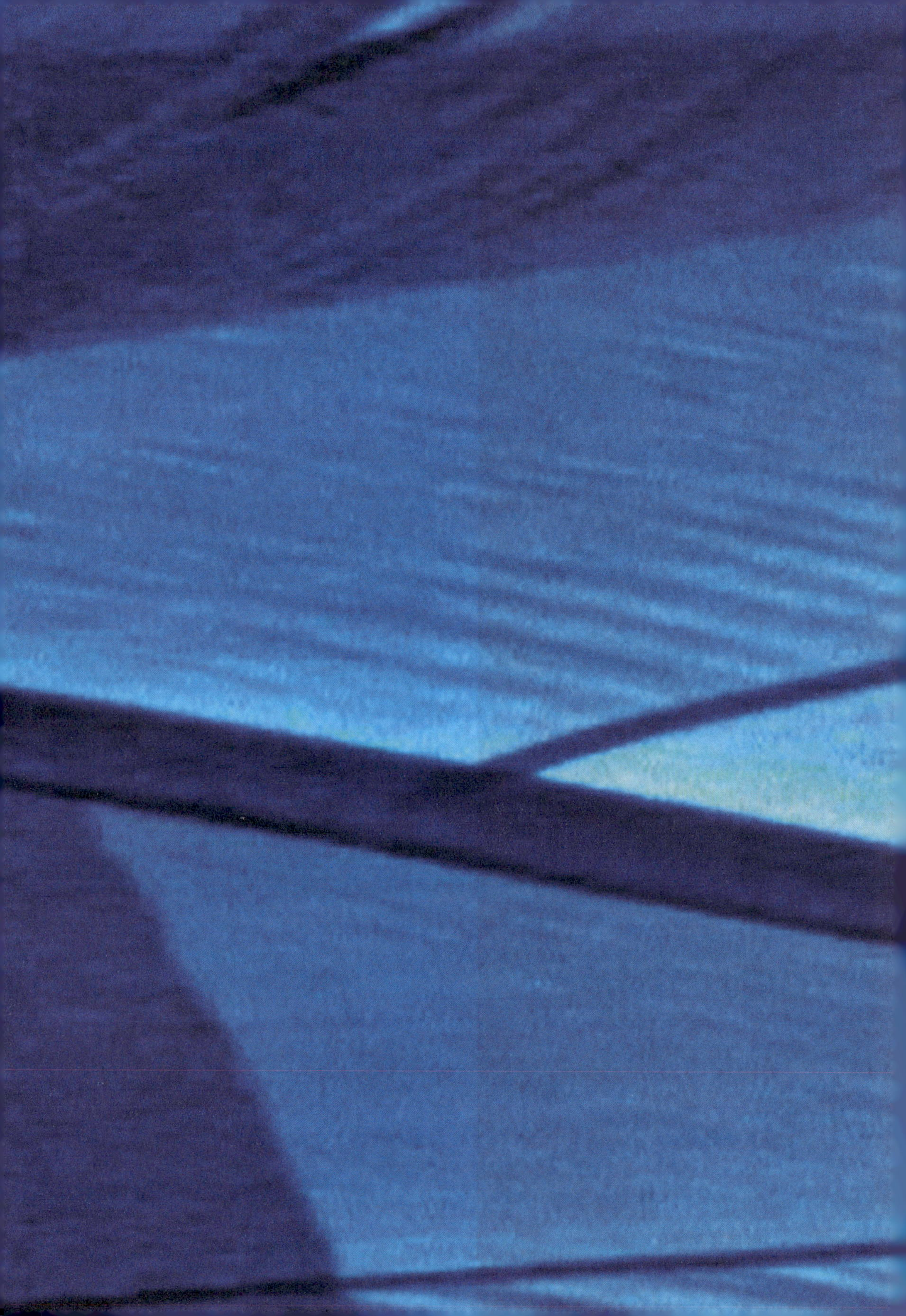

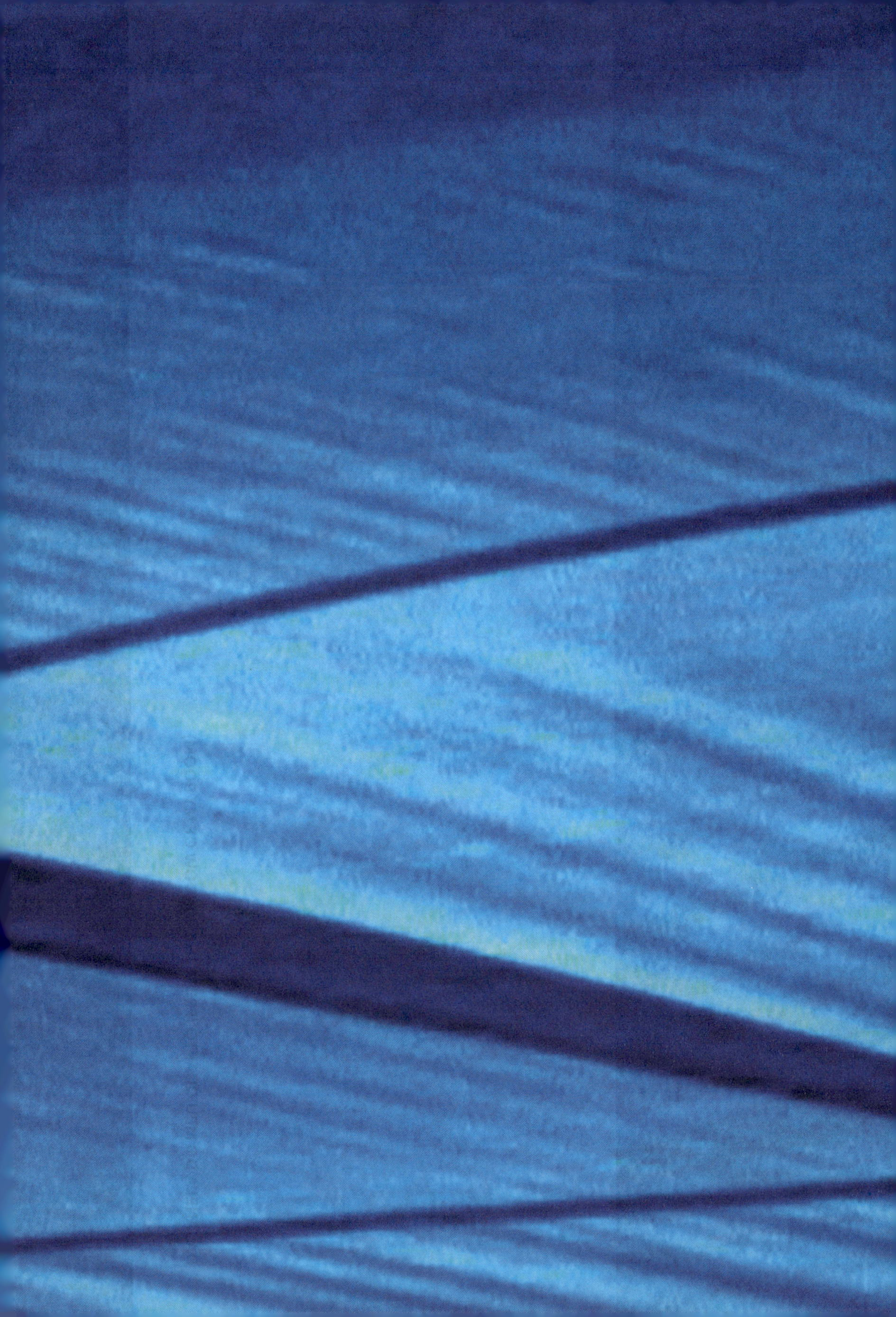

DA JANELA DO MEU QUARTO (FROM THE WINDOW OF MY ROOM) 2004

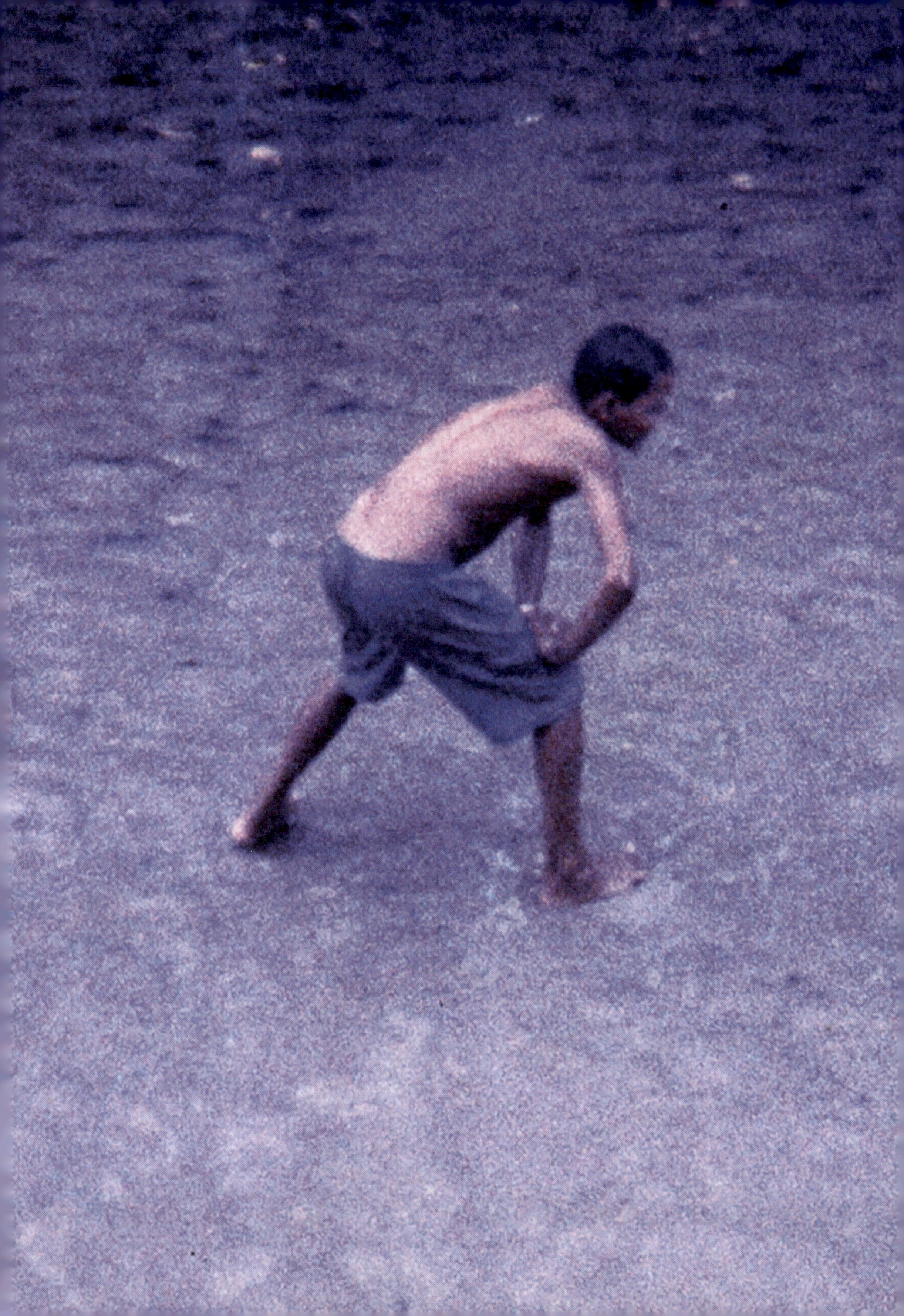

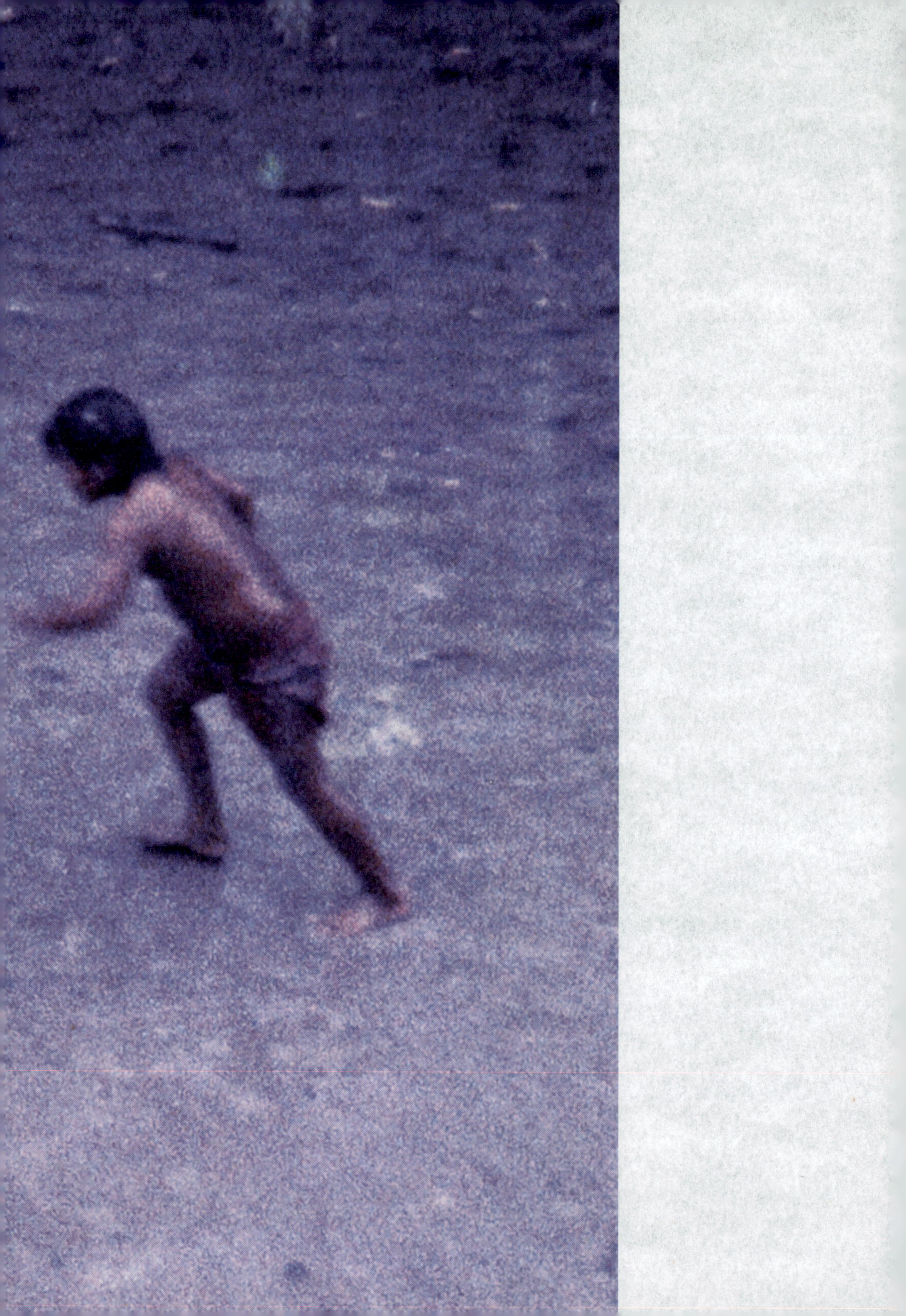

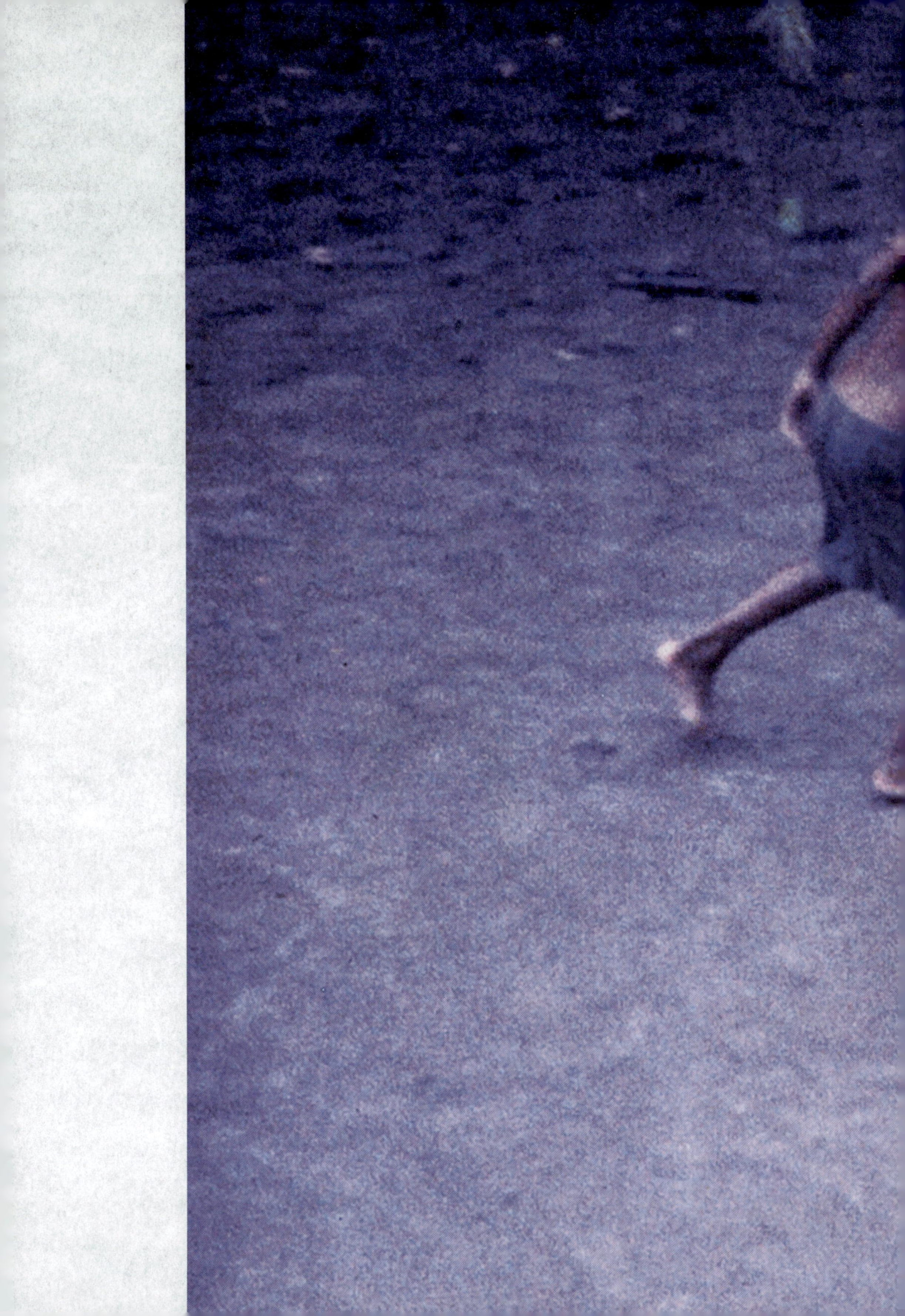

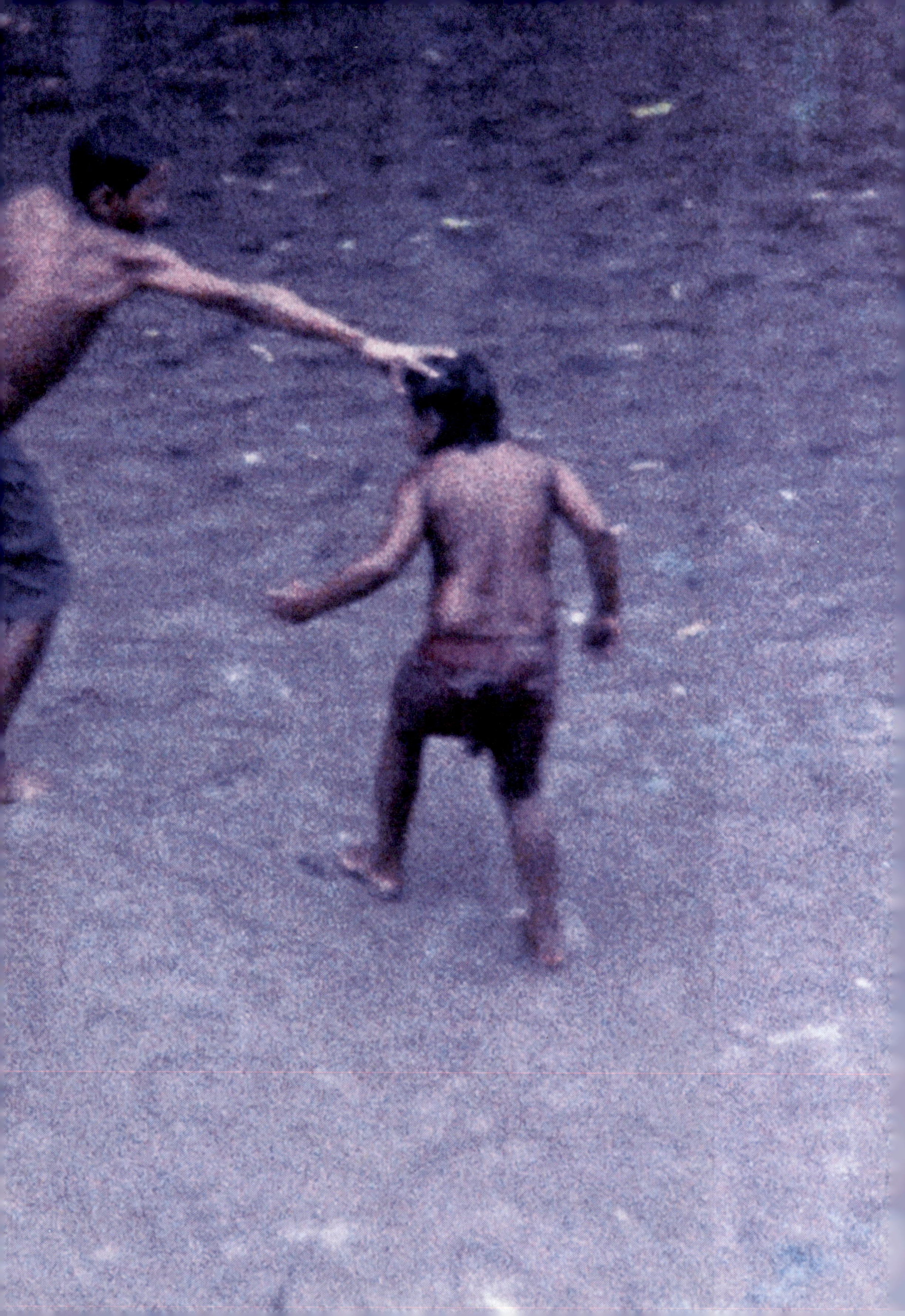

JOGO (GAME)   2016

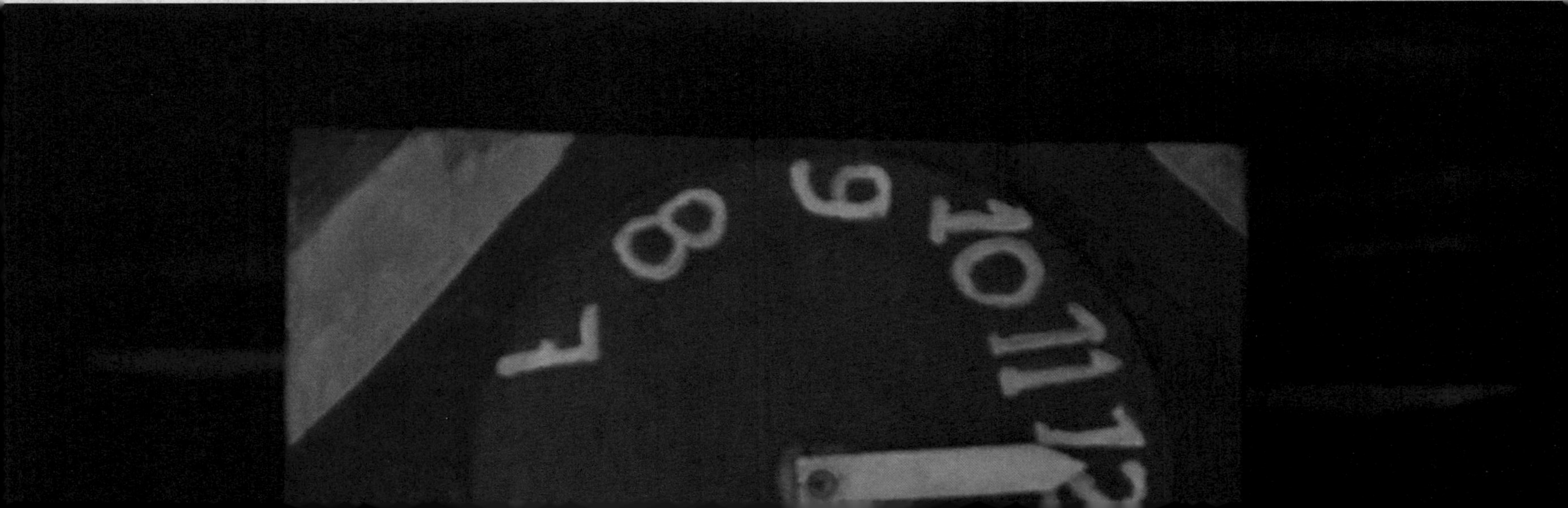

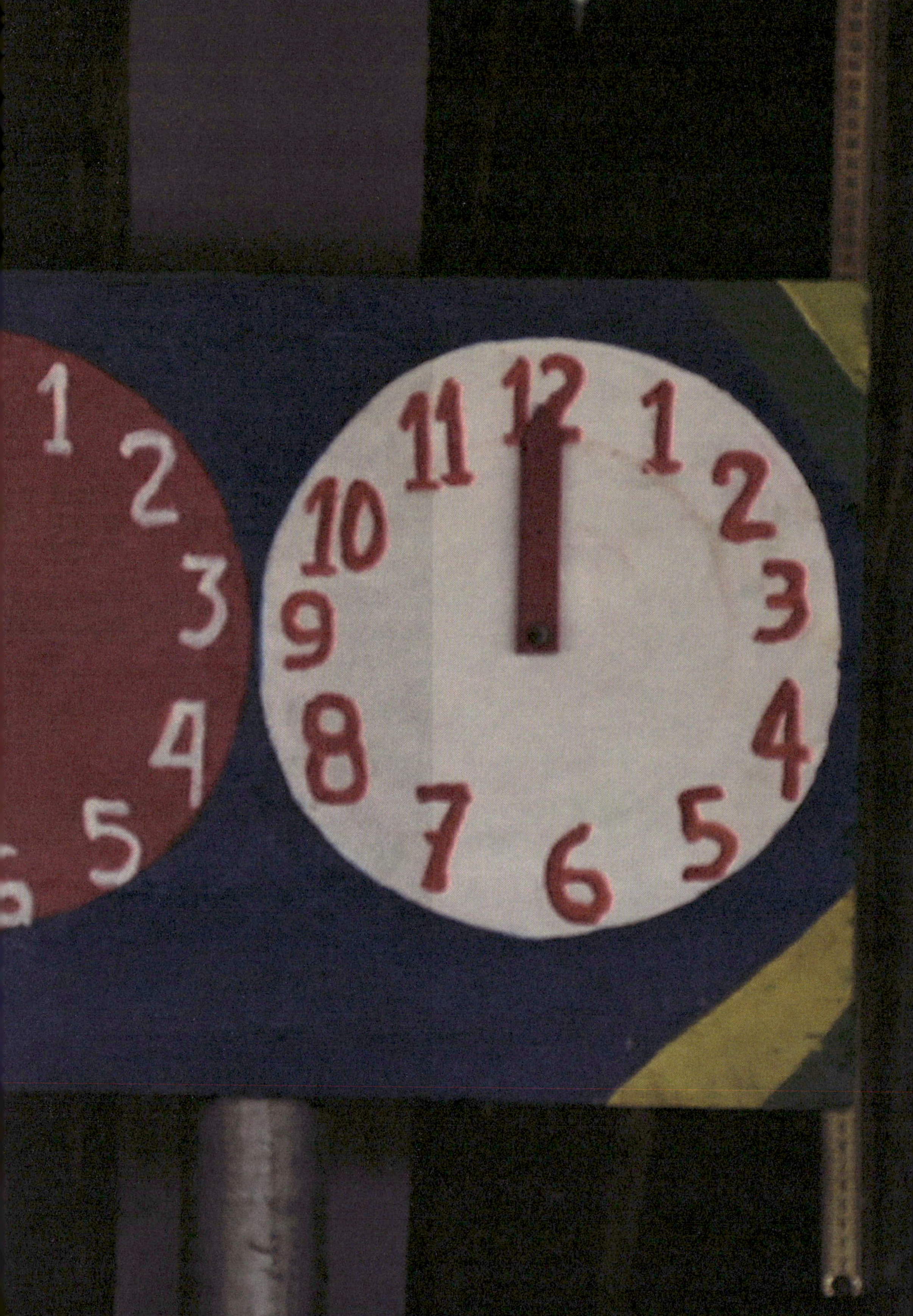
1
2
3
4
5
6
12 11 1
10 2
9 3
8 4
7 6 5
10
9
8
7

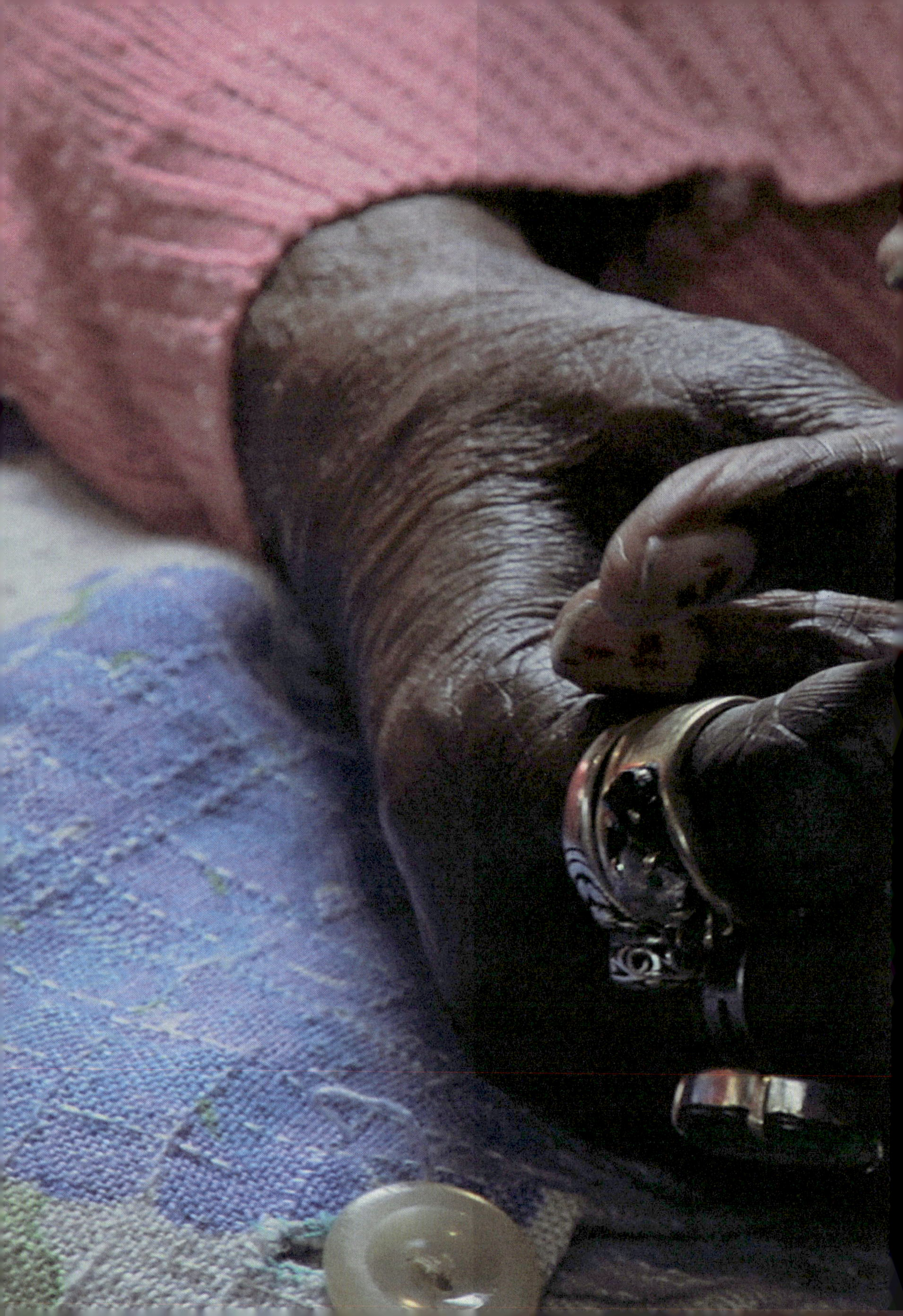

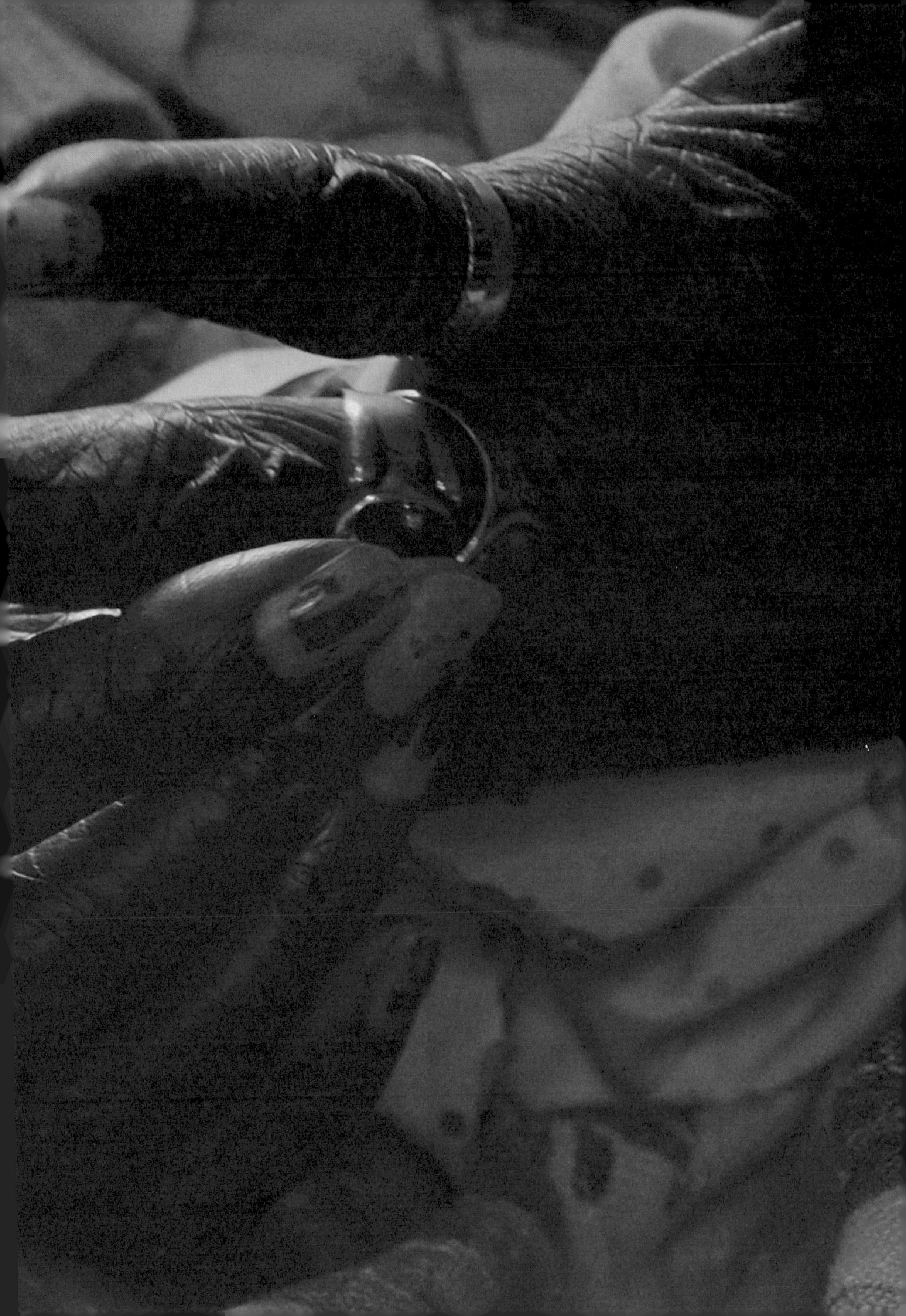

REZA (PRAYER)   2016

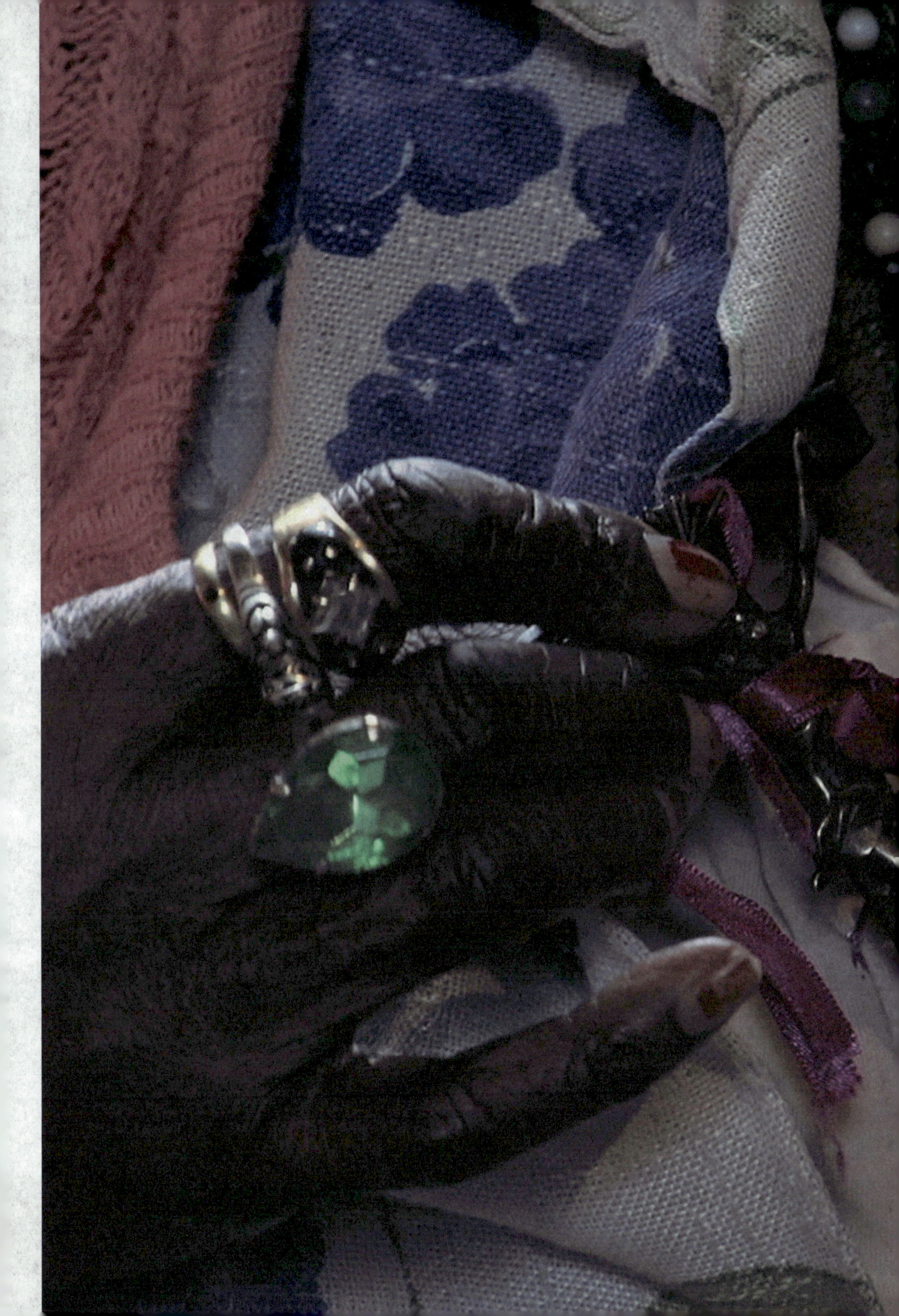

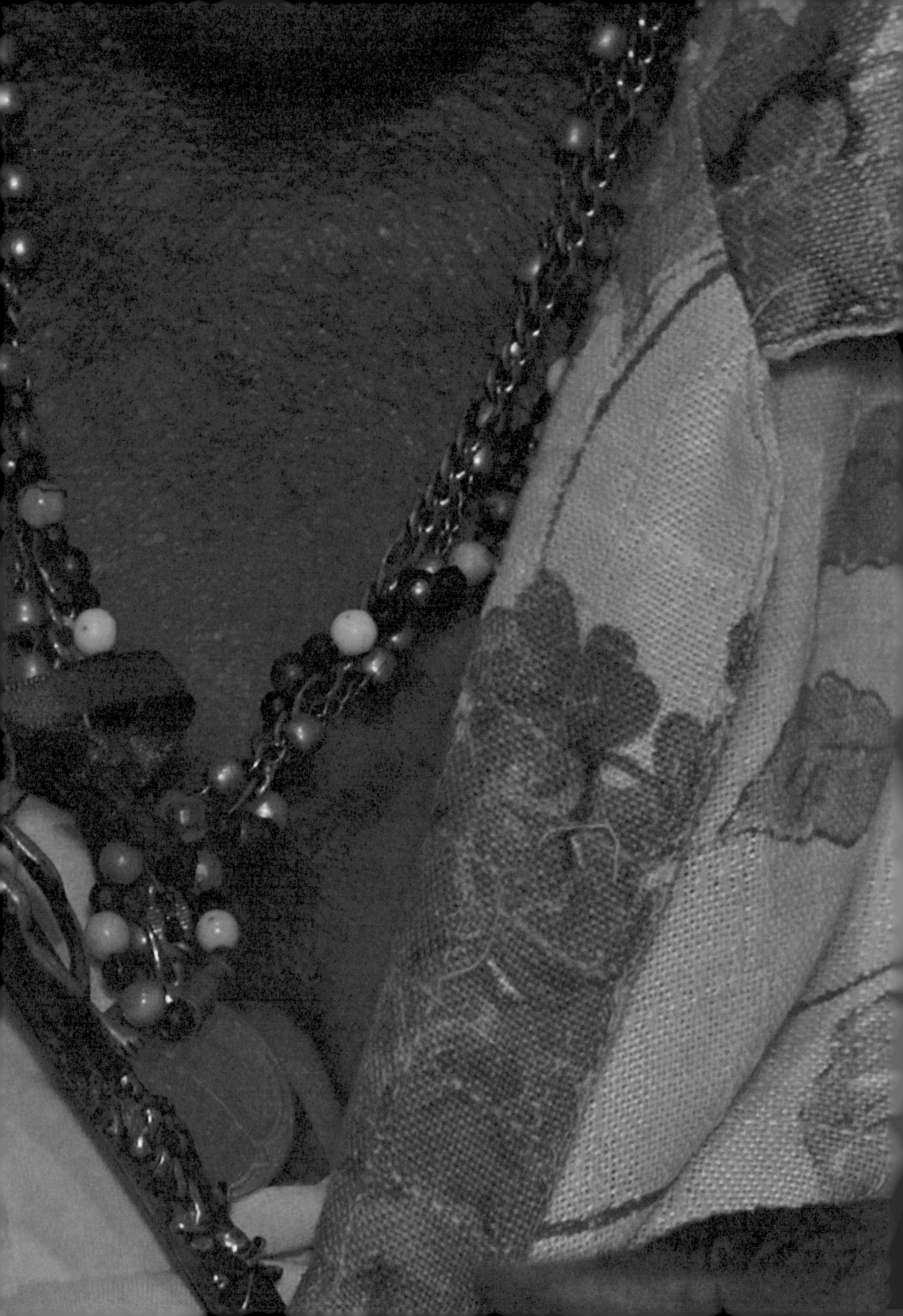

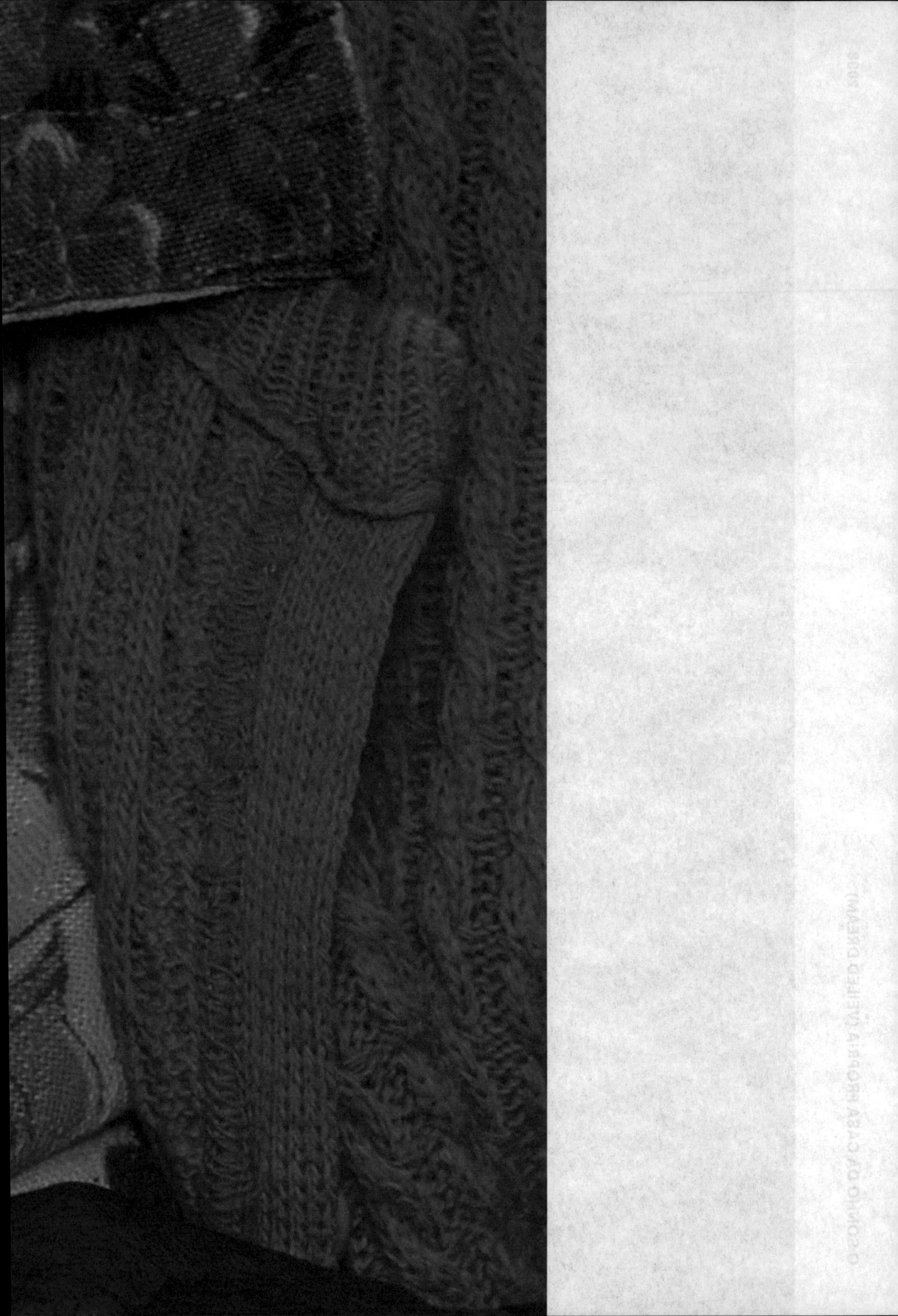

O SONHO DA CASA PRÓPRIA (VEILED DREAM)   2008

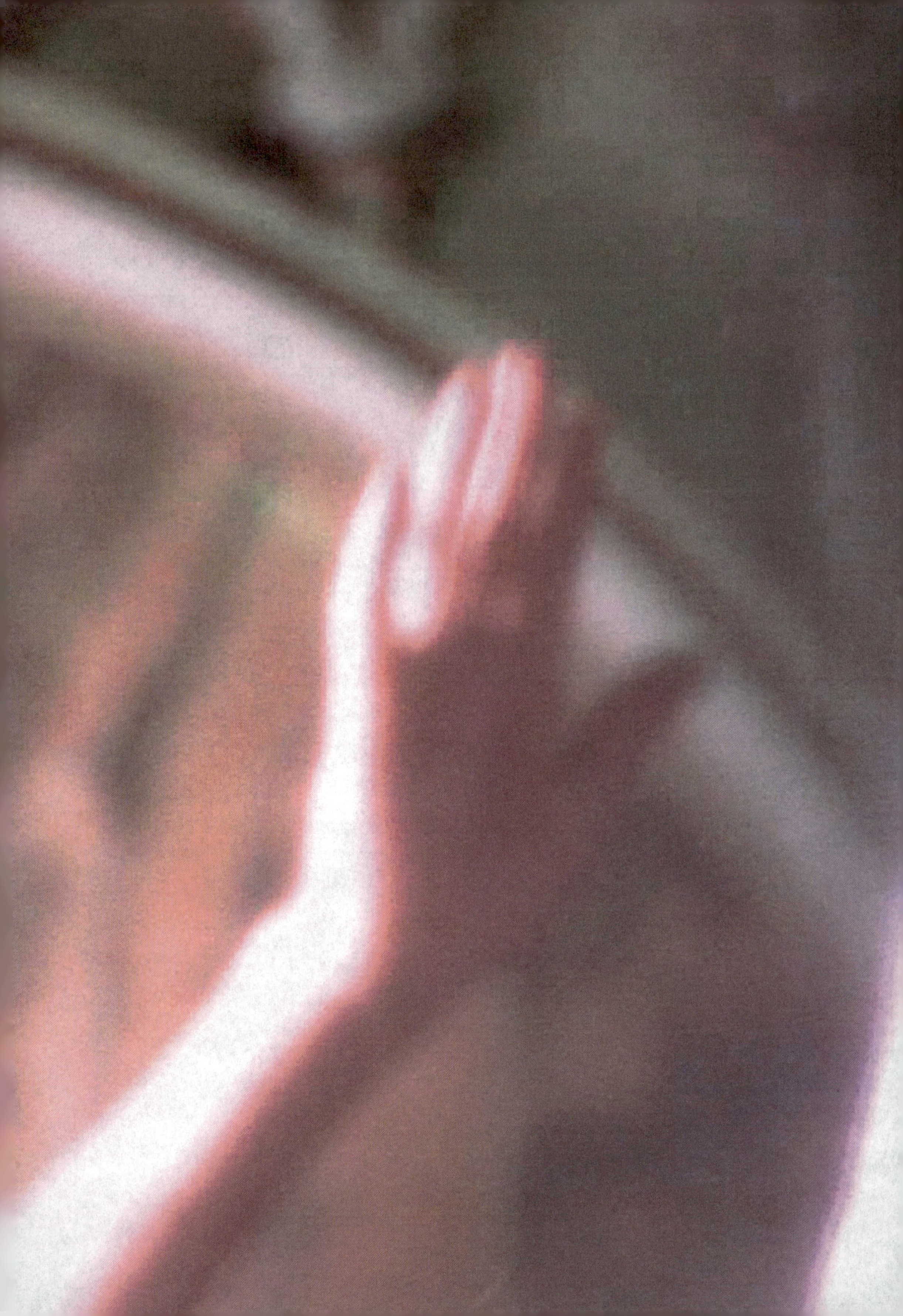

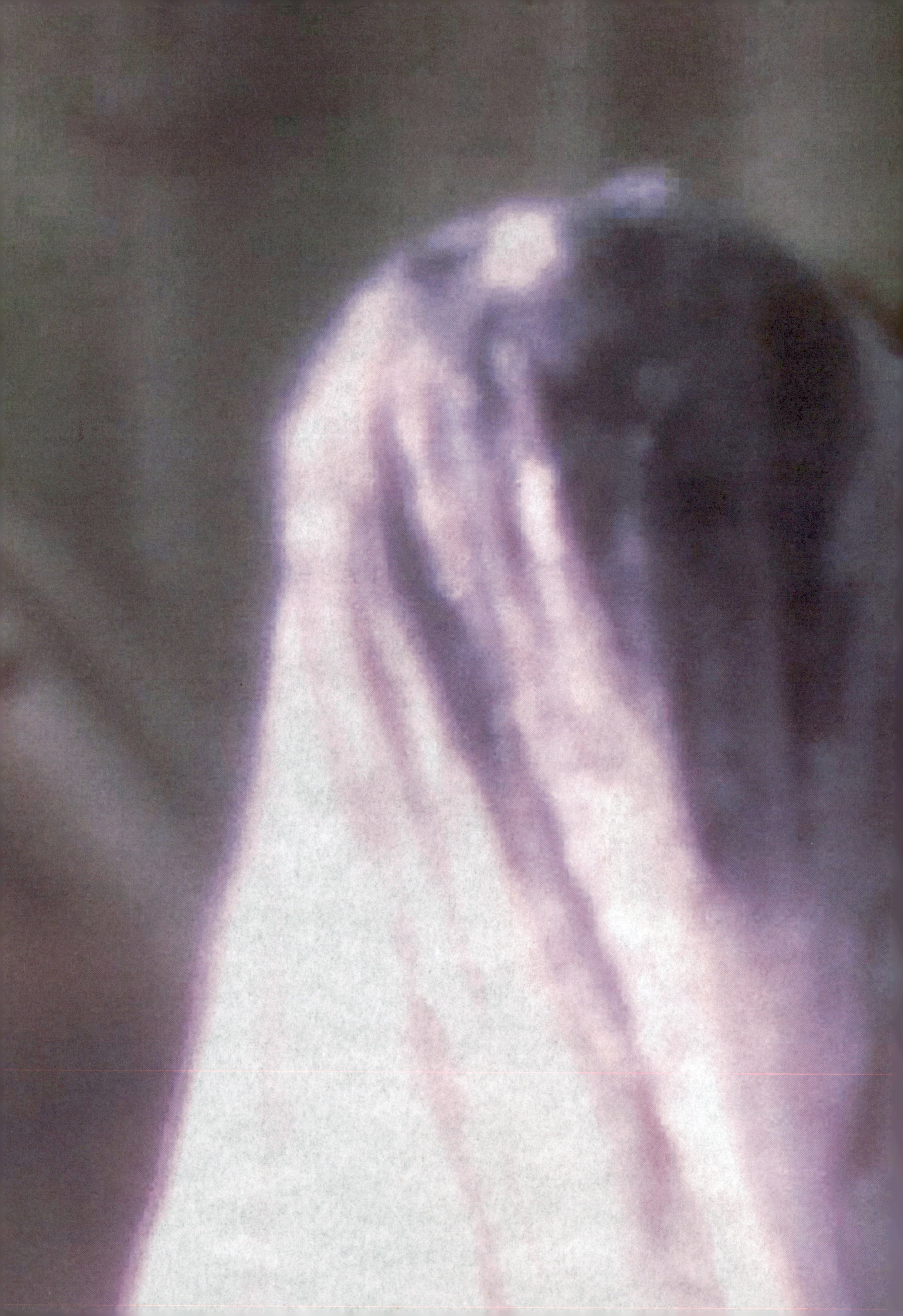

QUARTA-FEIRA DE CINZAS (EPILOGUE: ASH WEDNESDAY)

2006

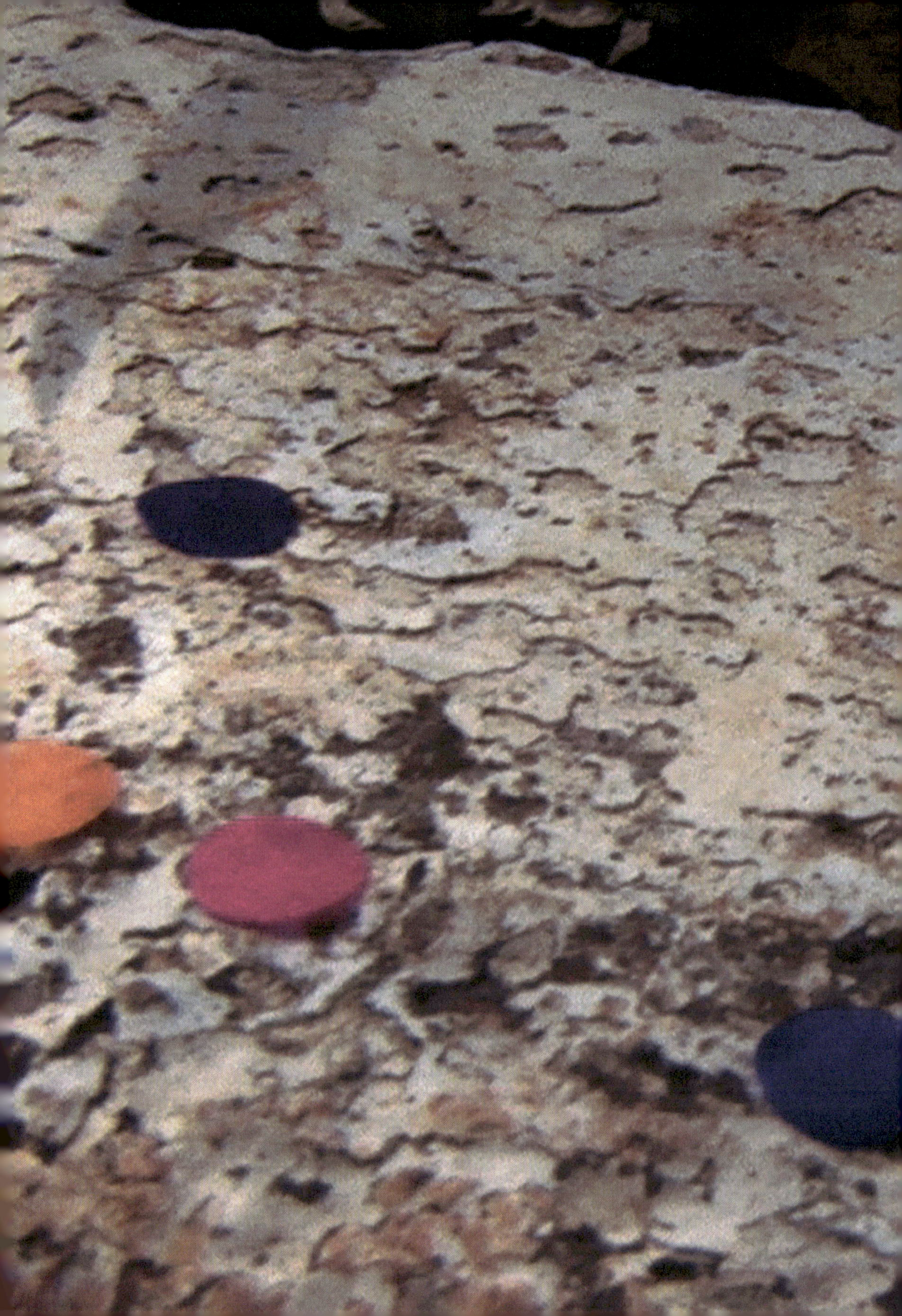

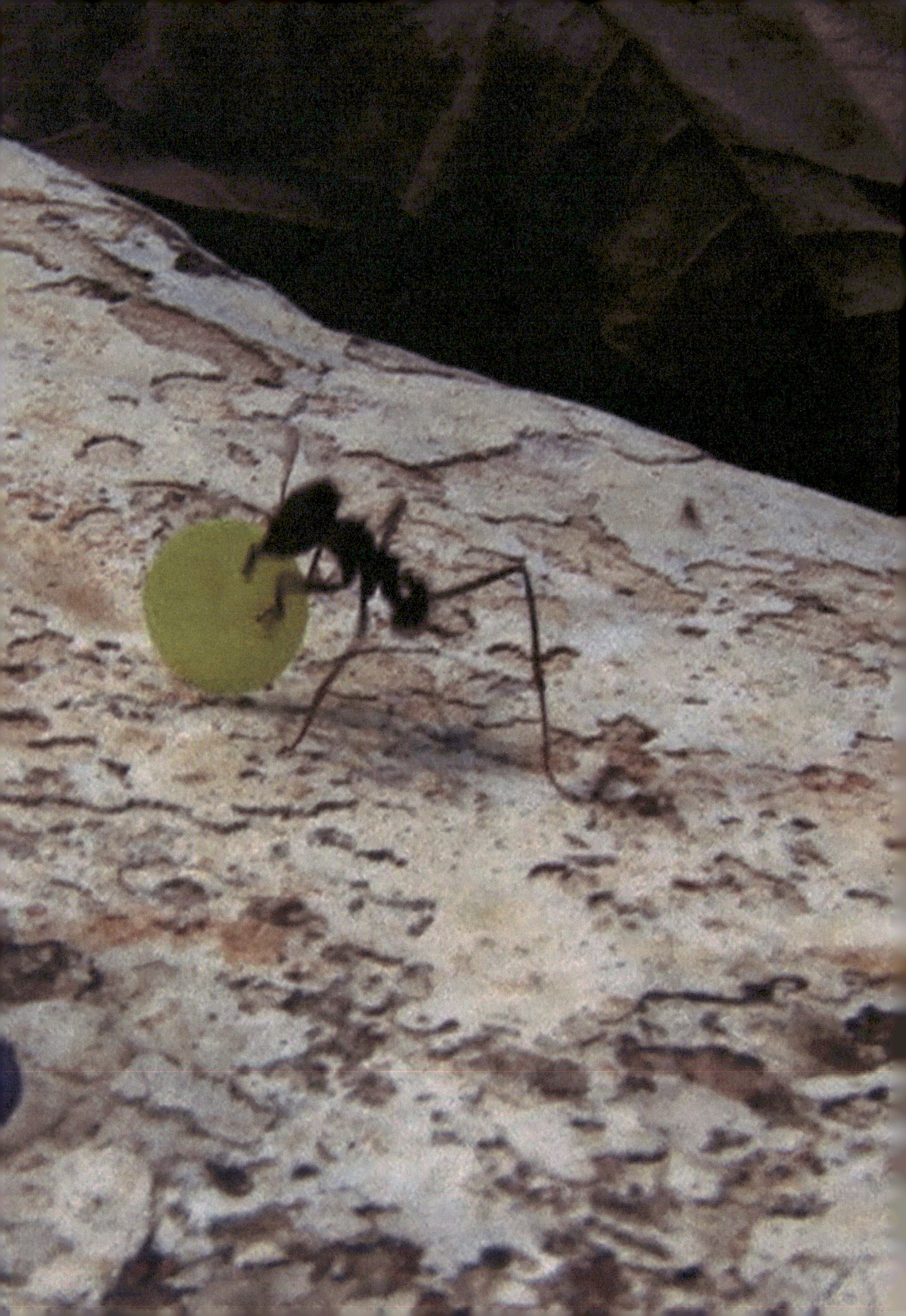

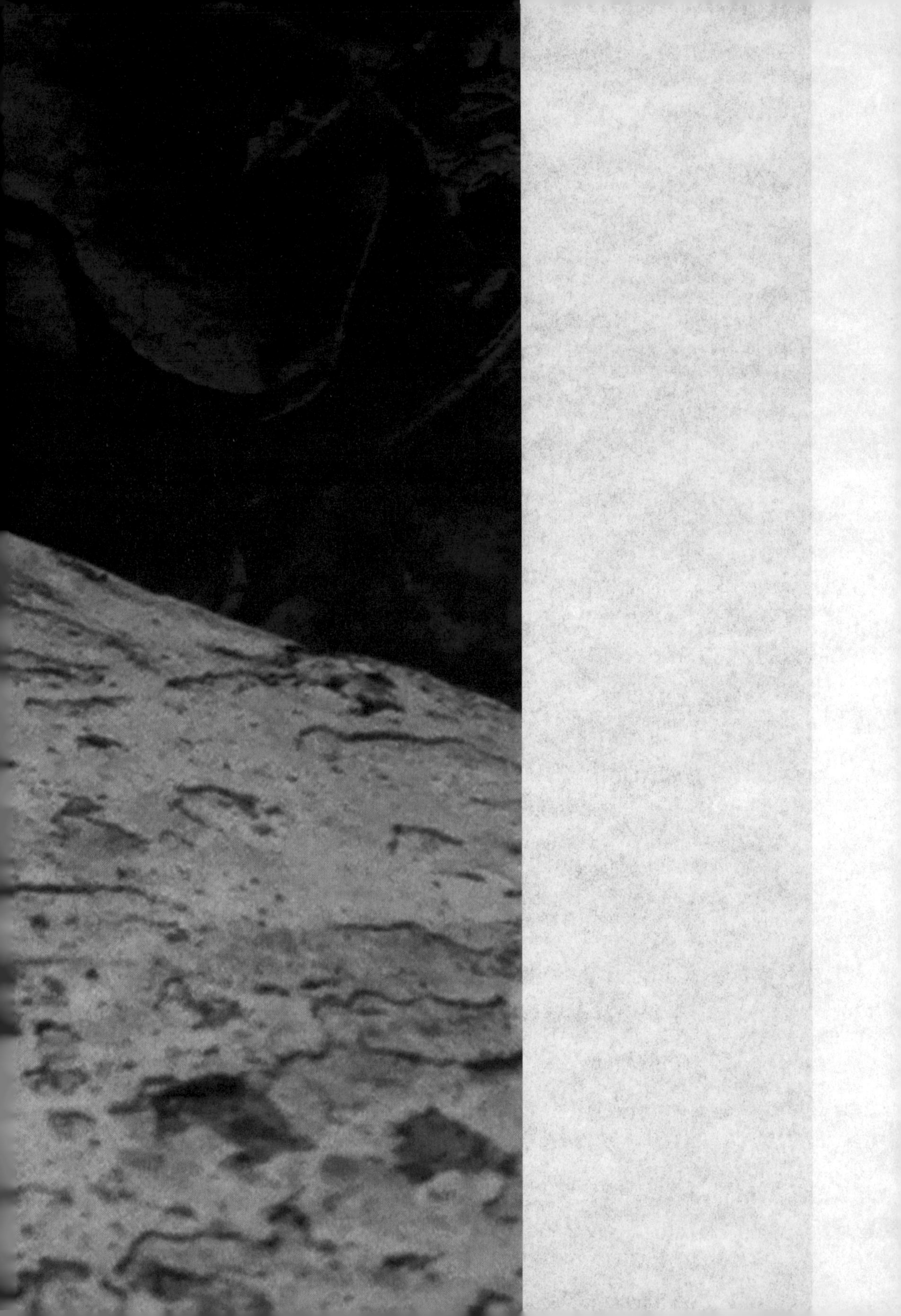

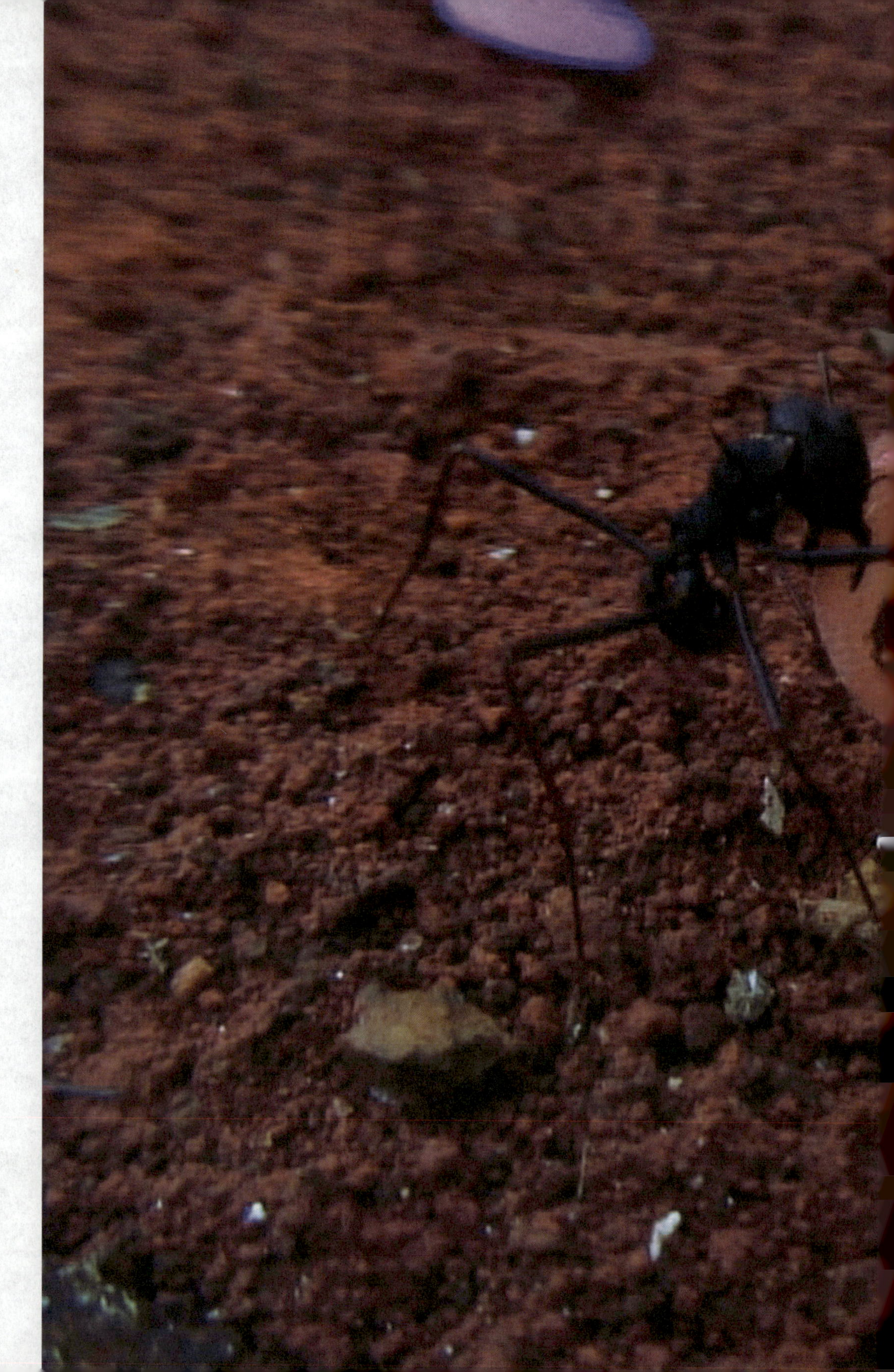

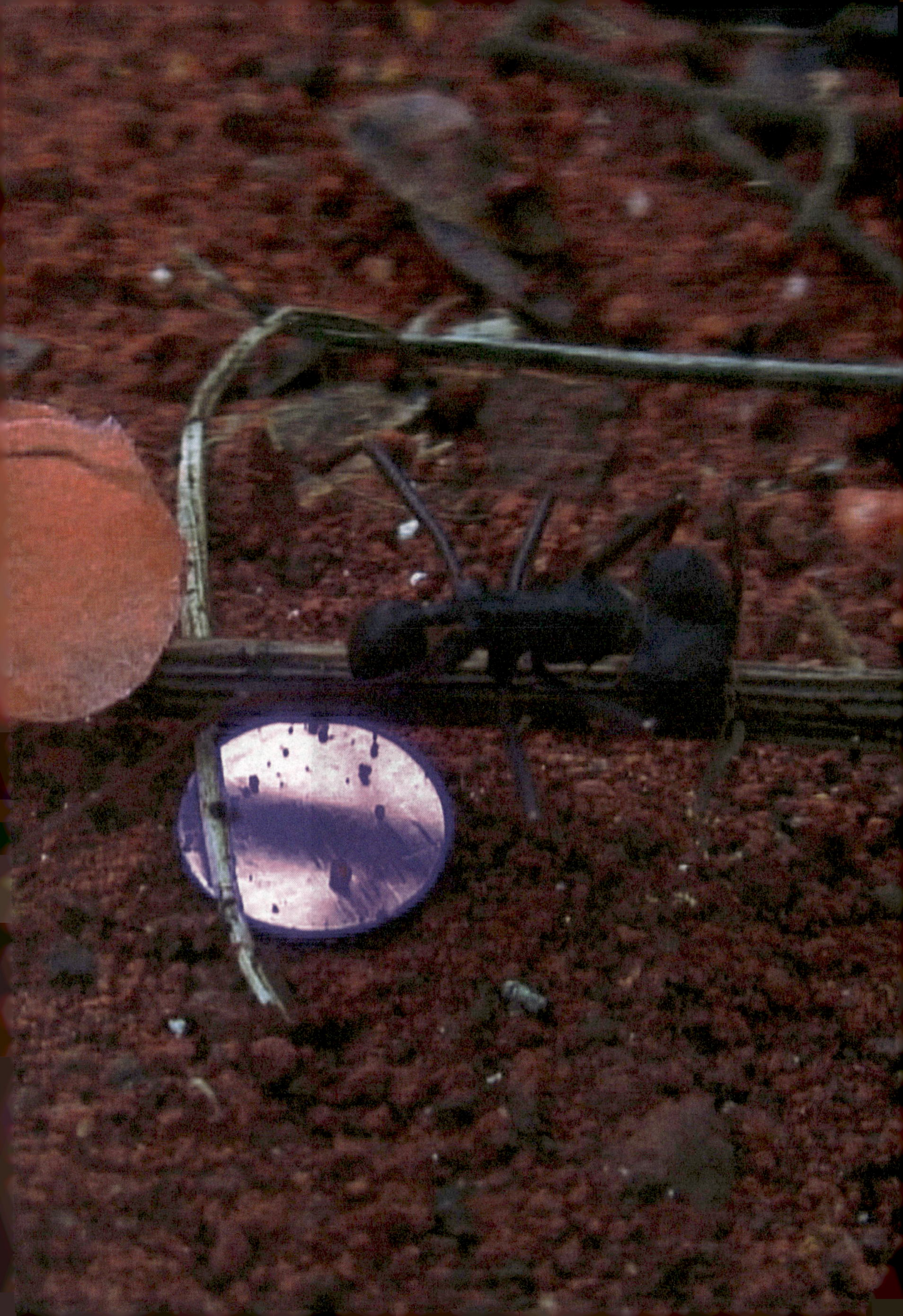

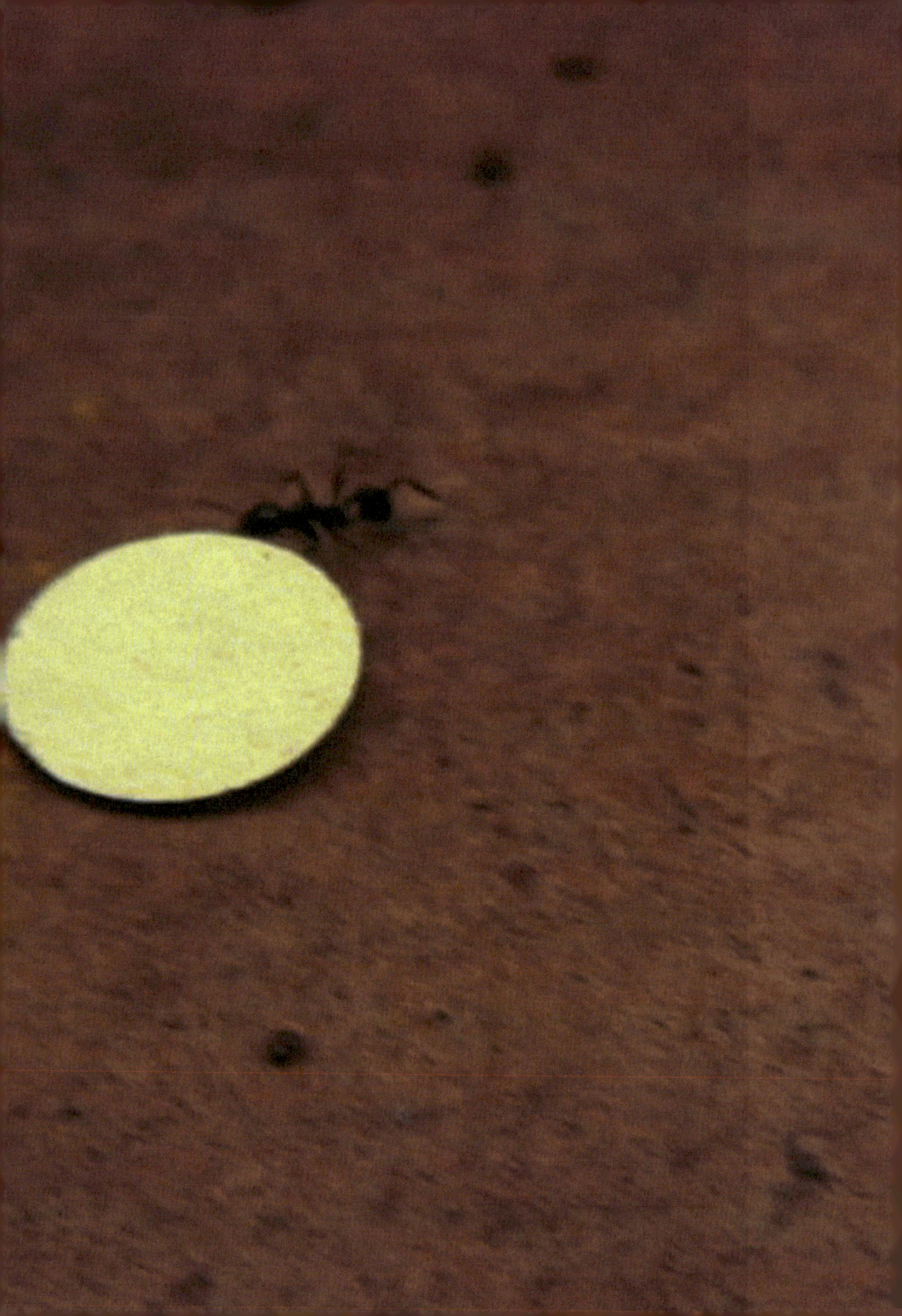

SOPRO (BLOW) 2000

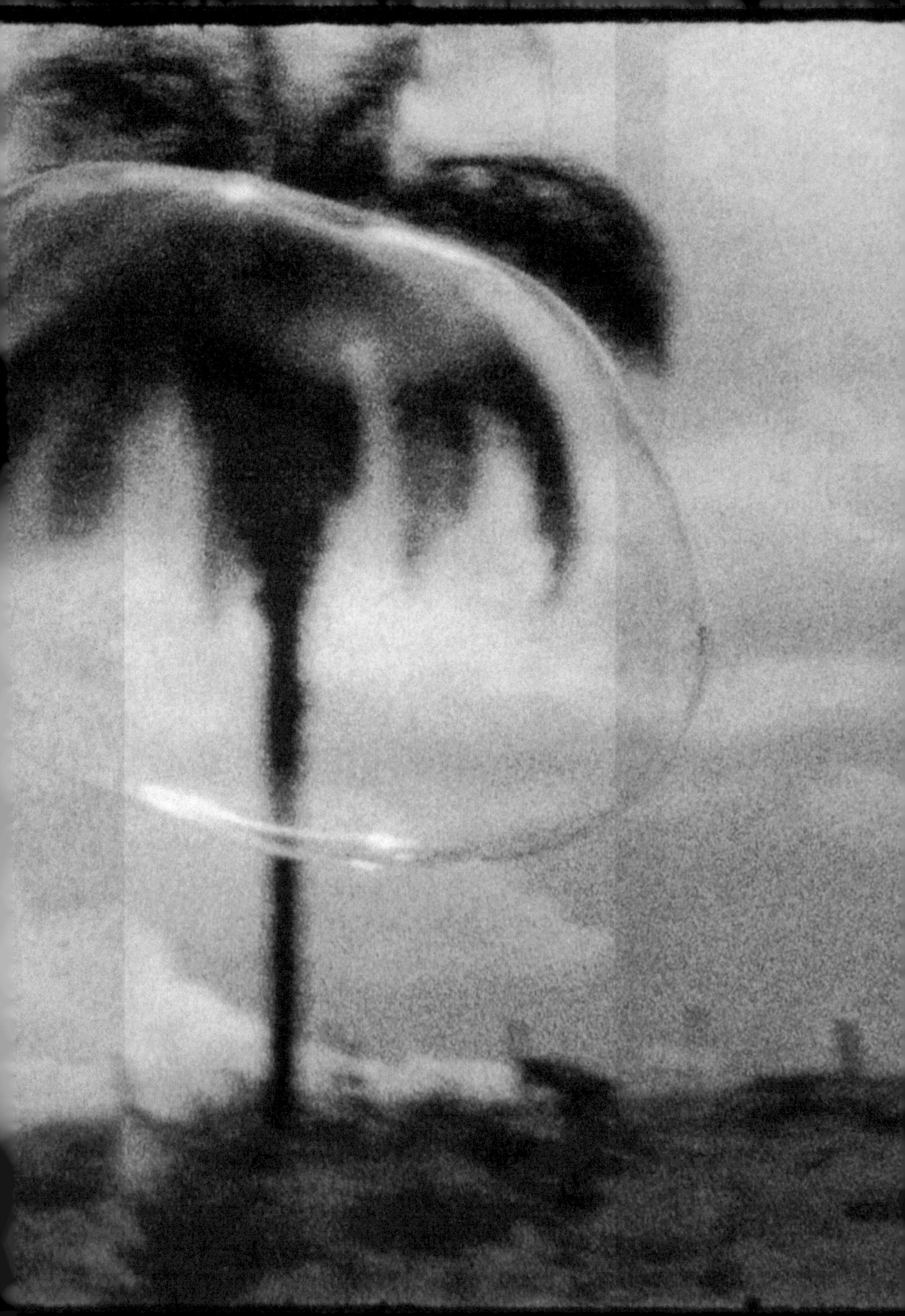

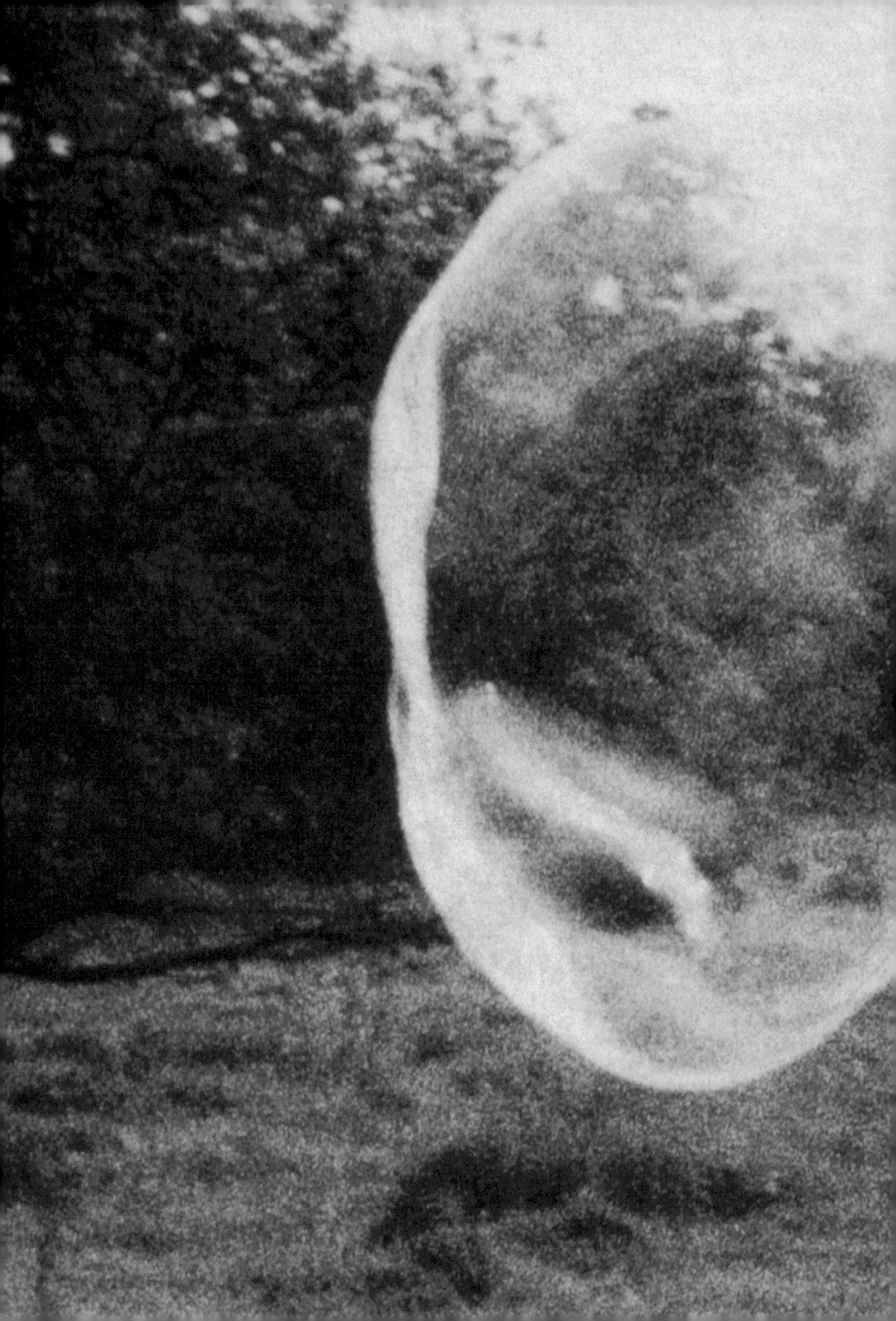

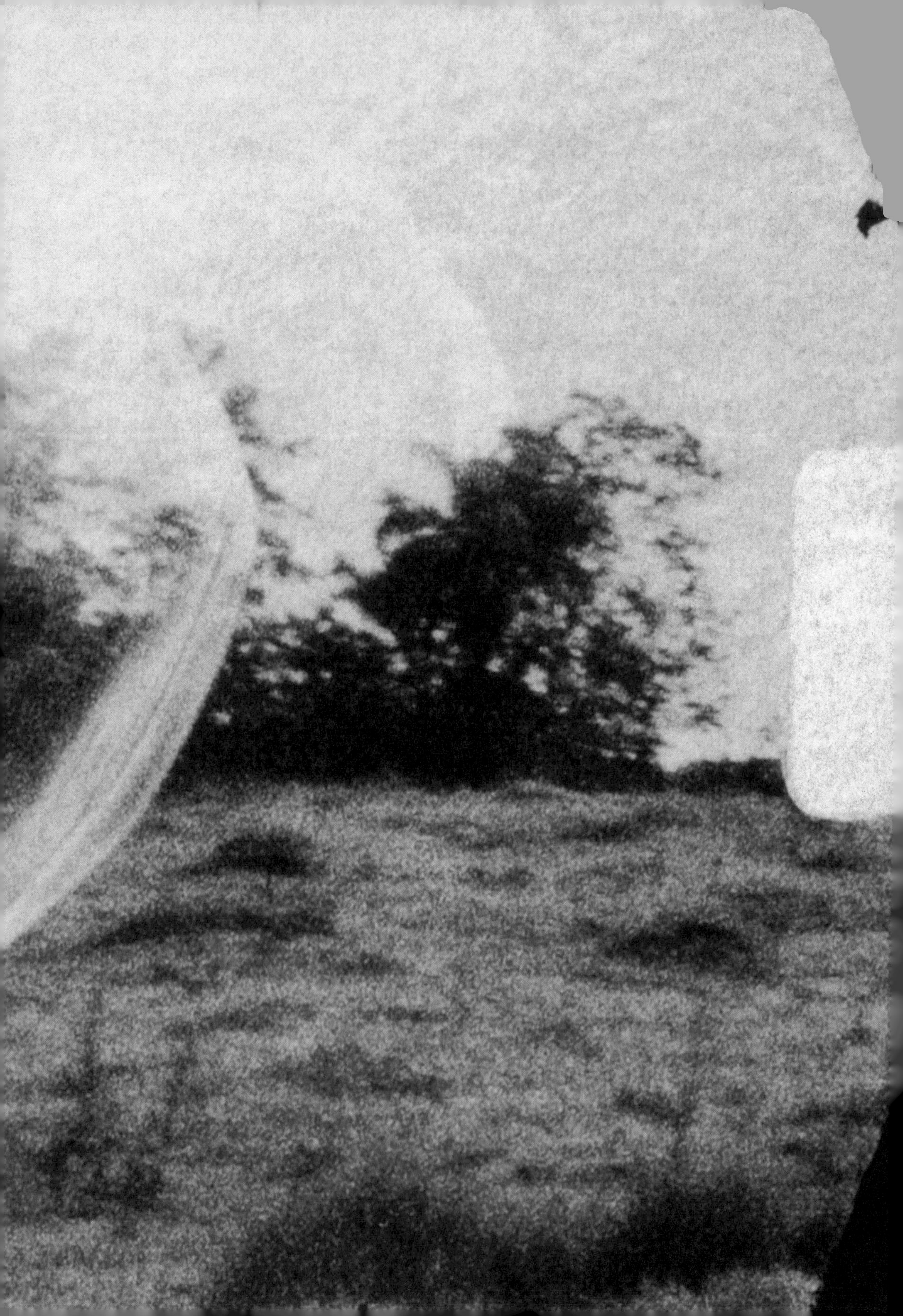

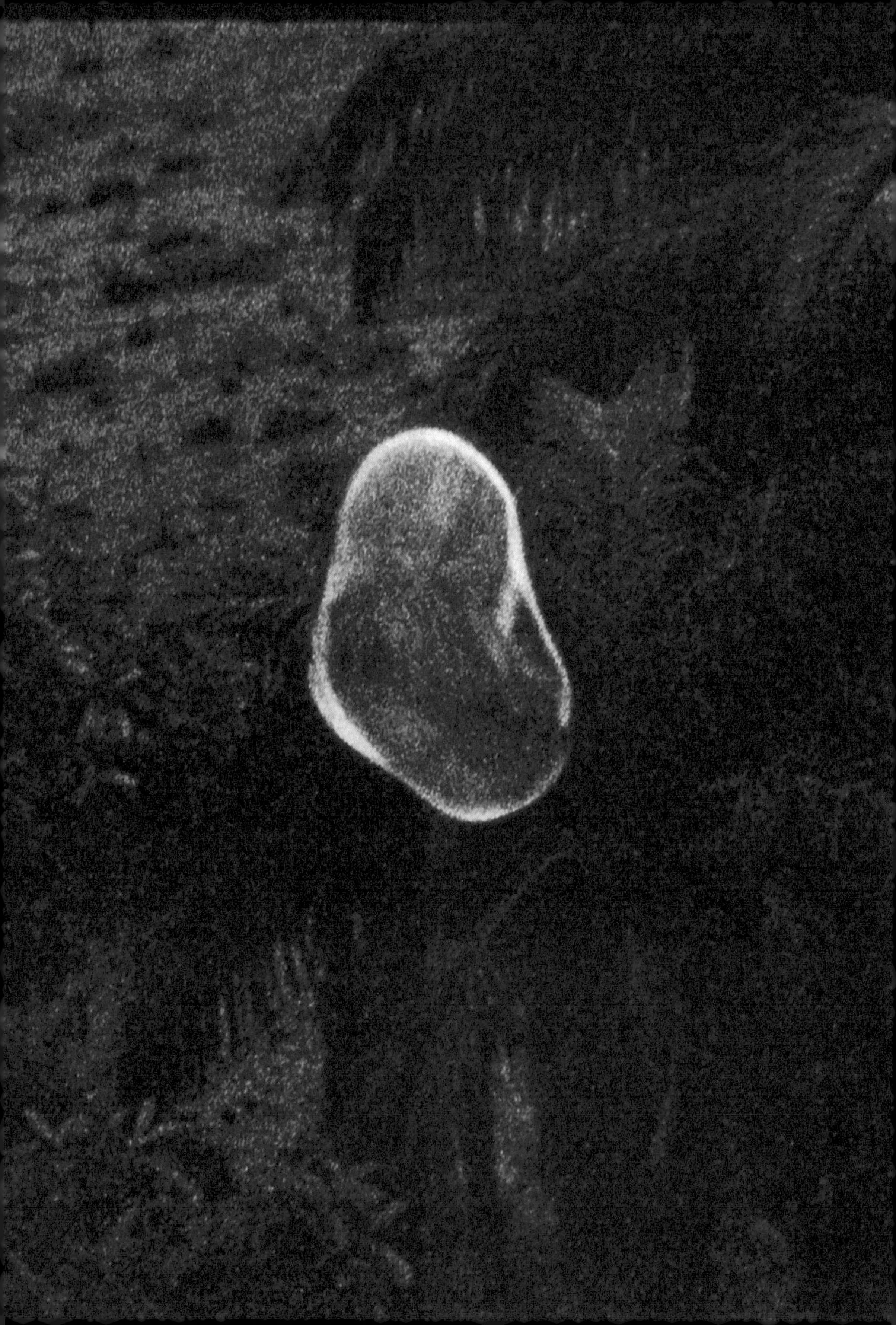

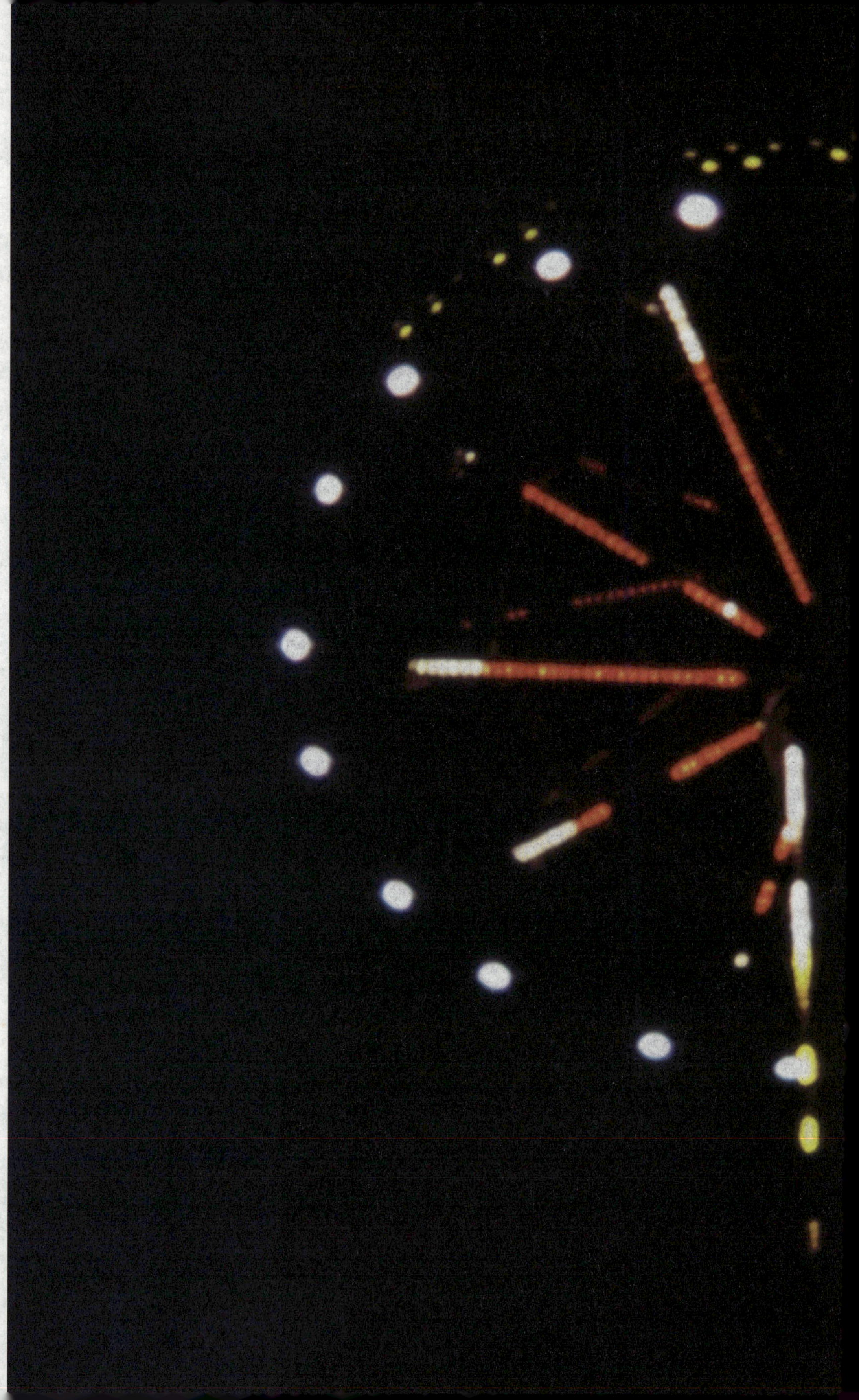

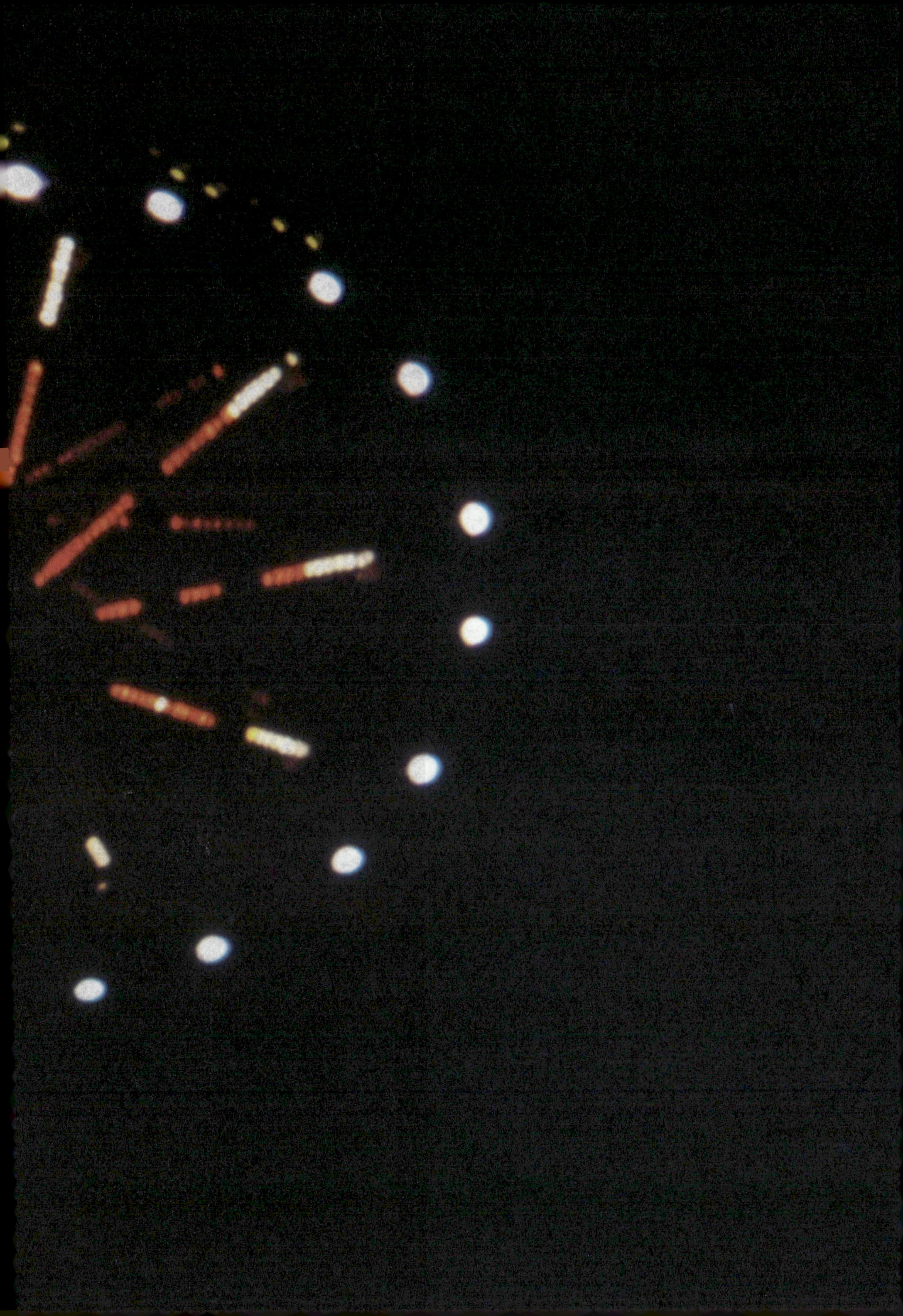

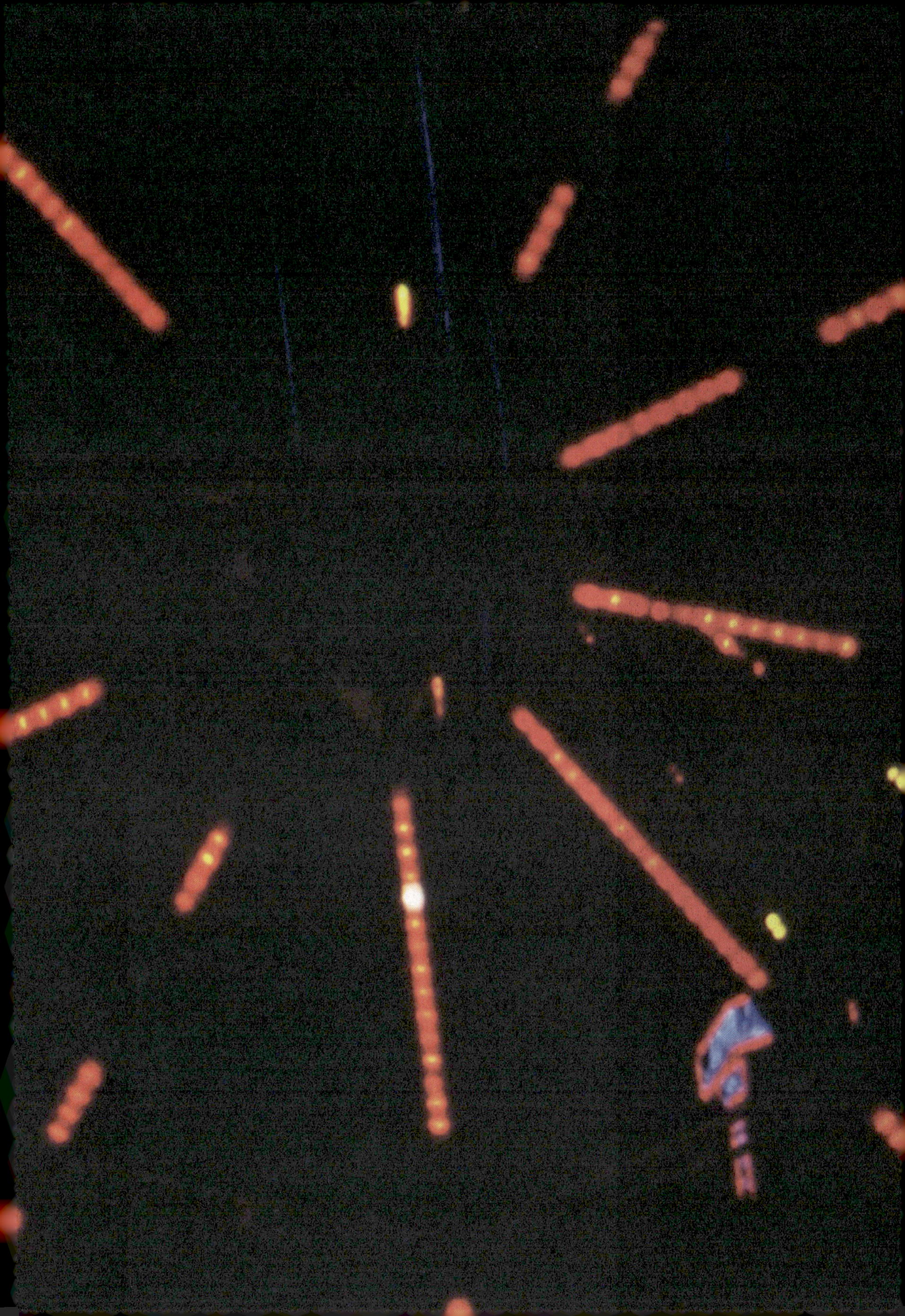

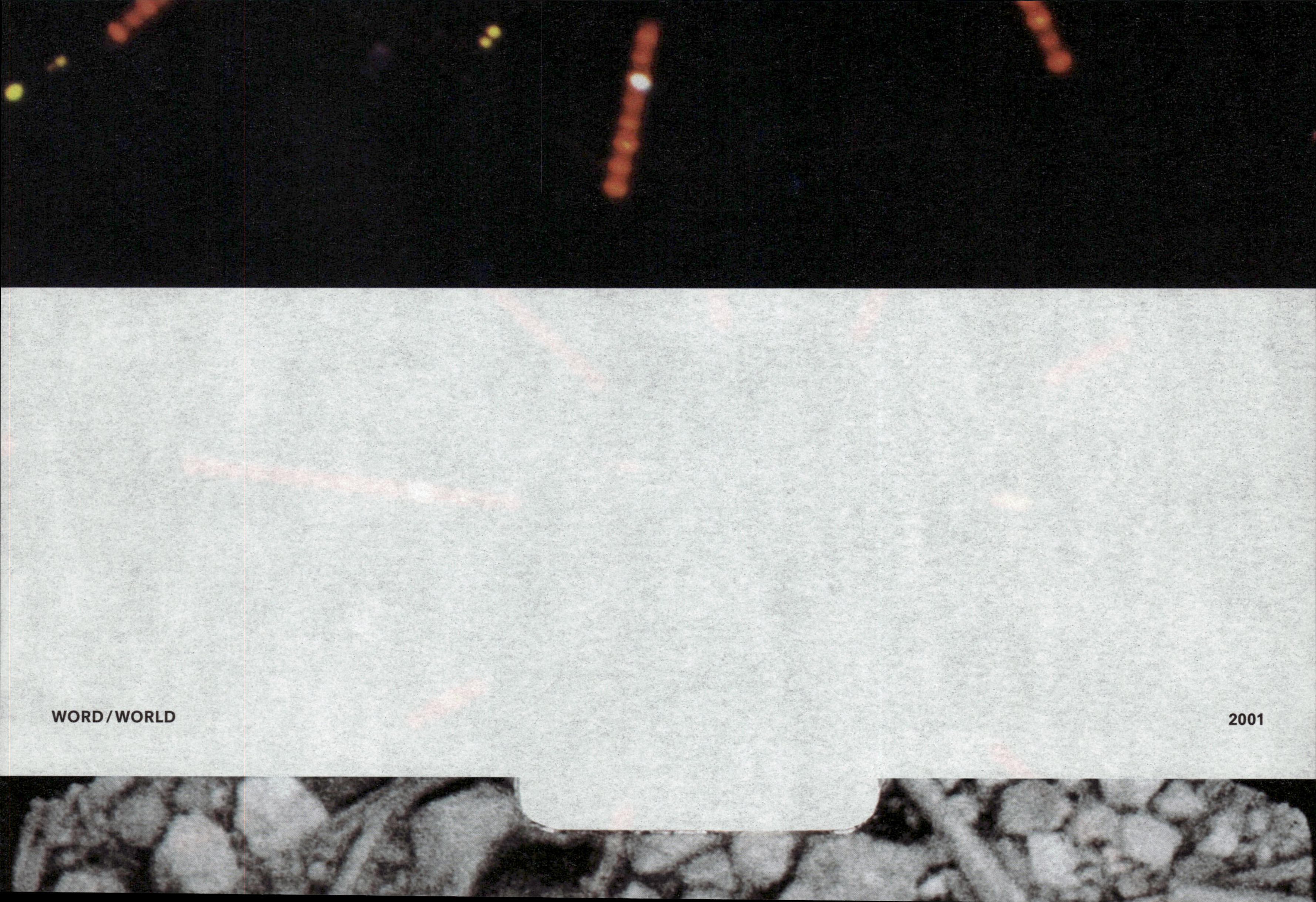

WORD / WORLD   2001

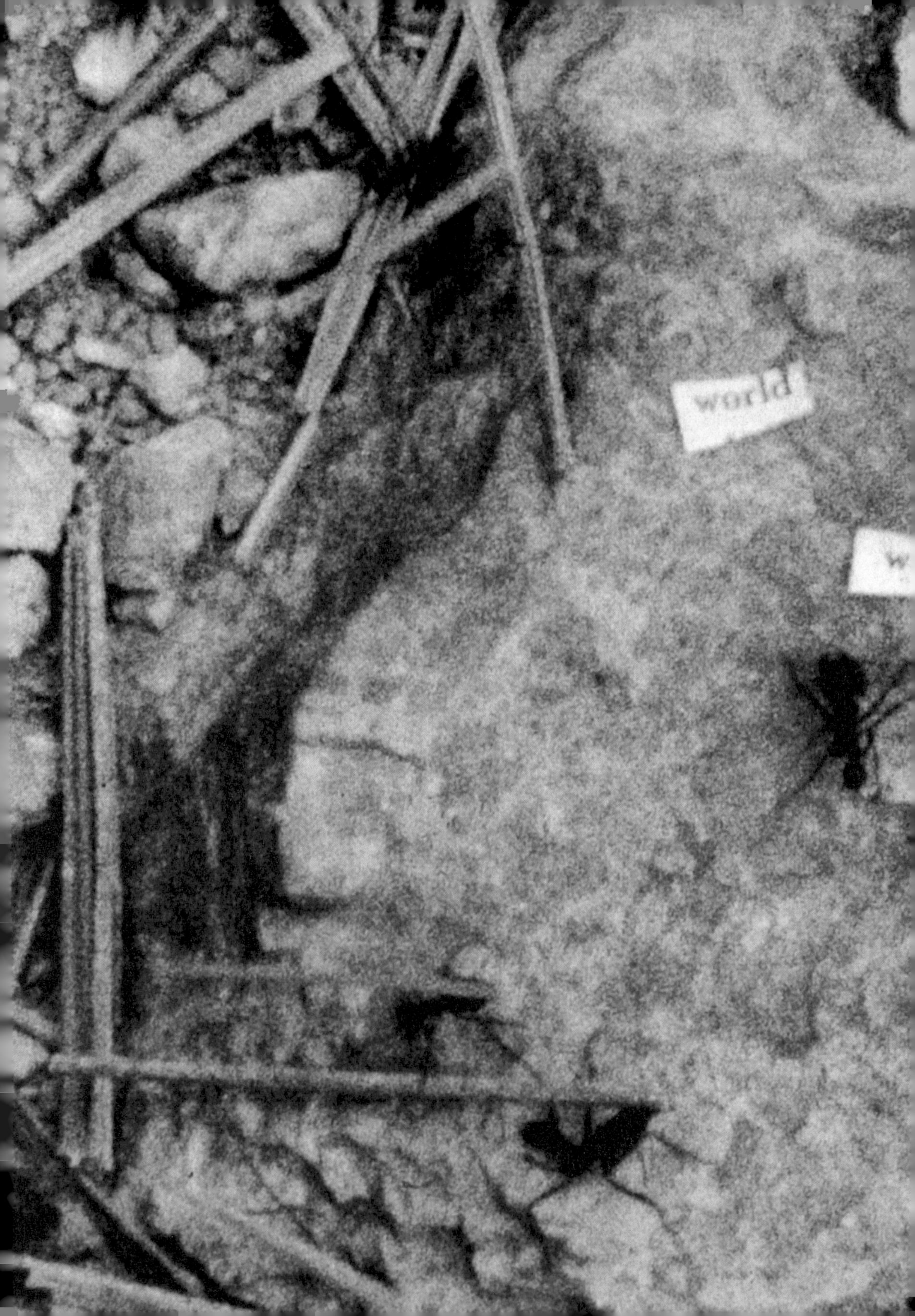
world
w

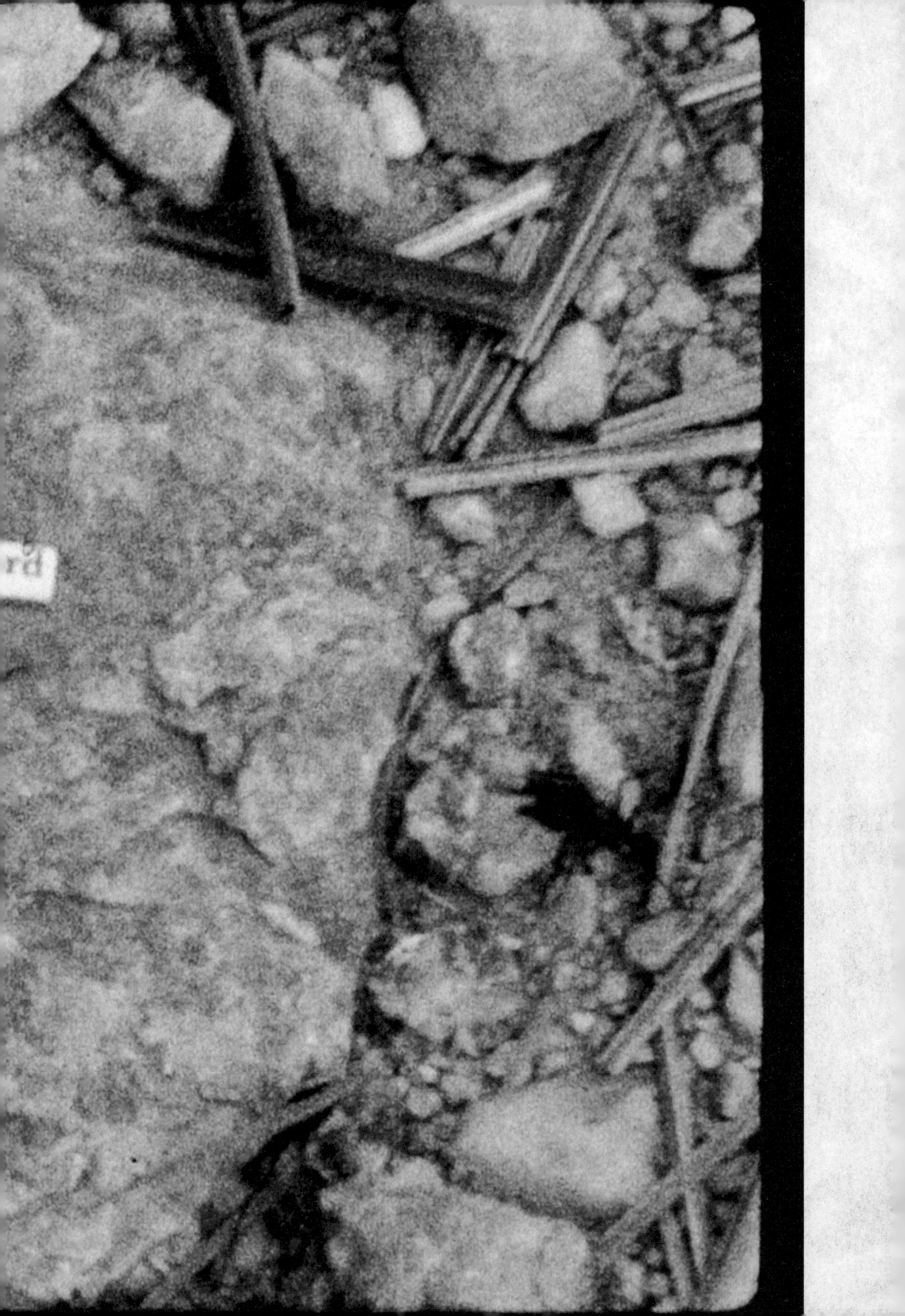

O INQUILINO (THE TENANT)	2010

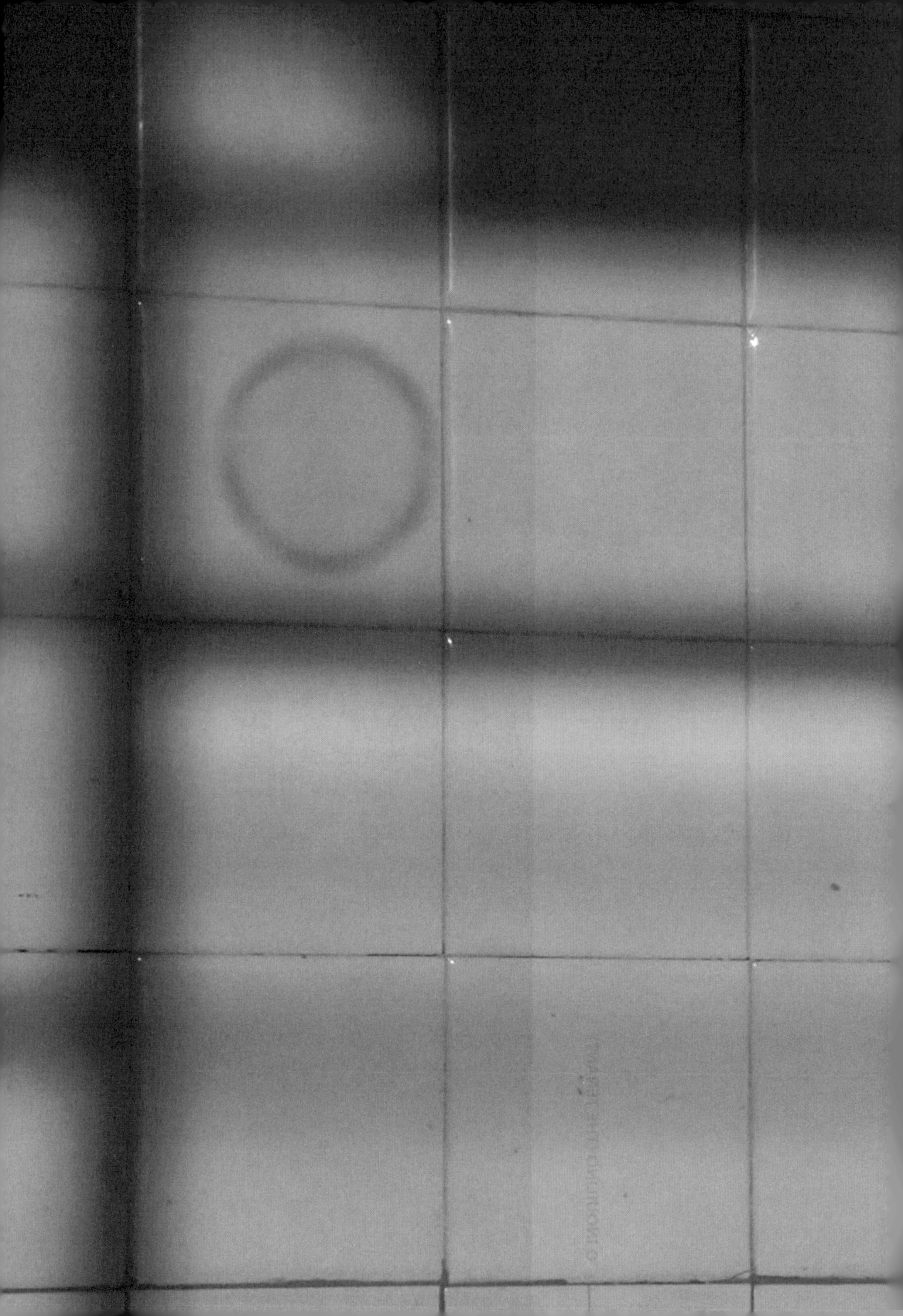

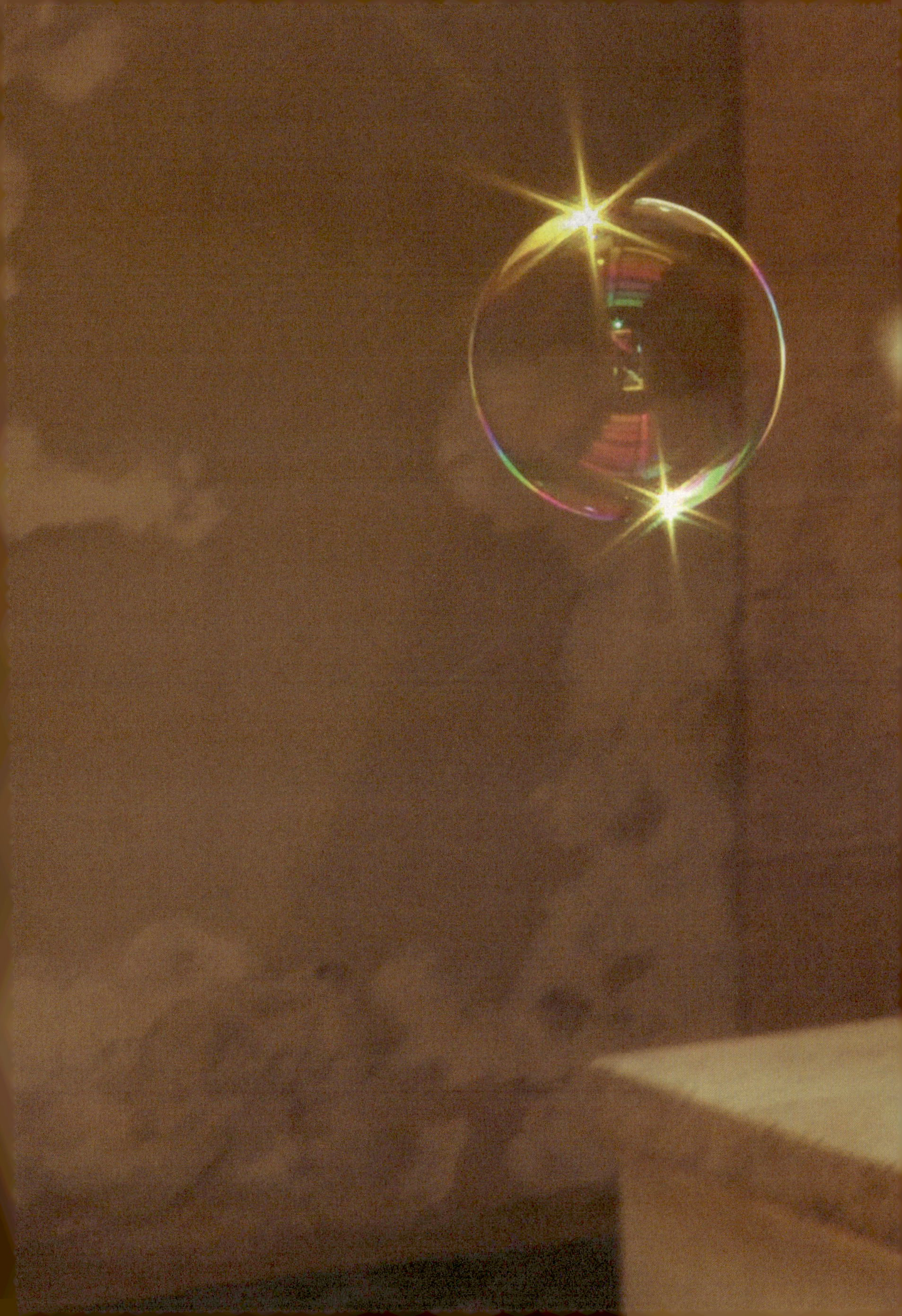

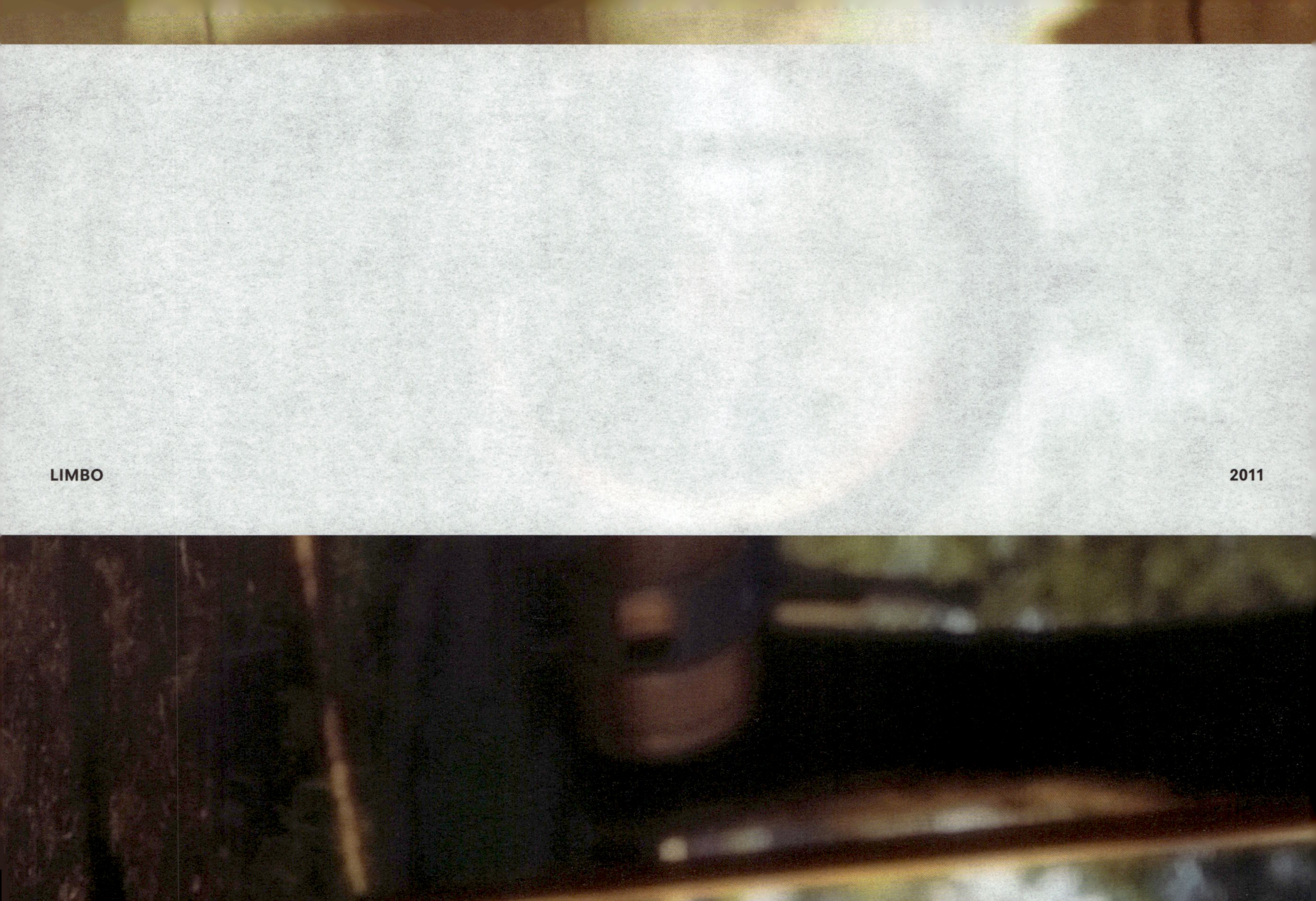
LIMBO
2011

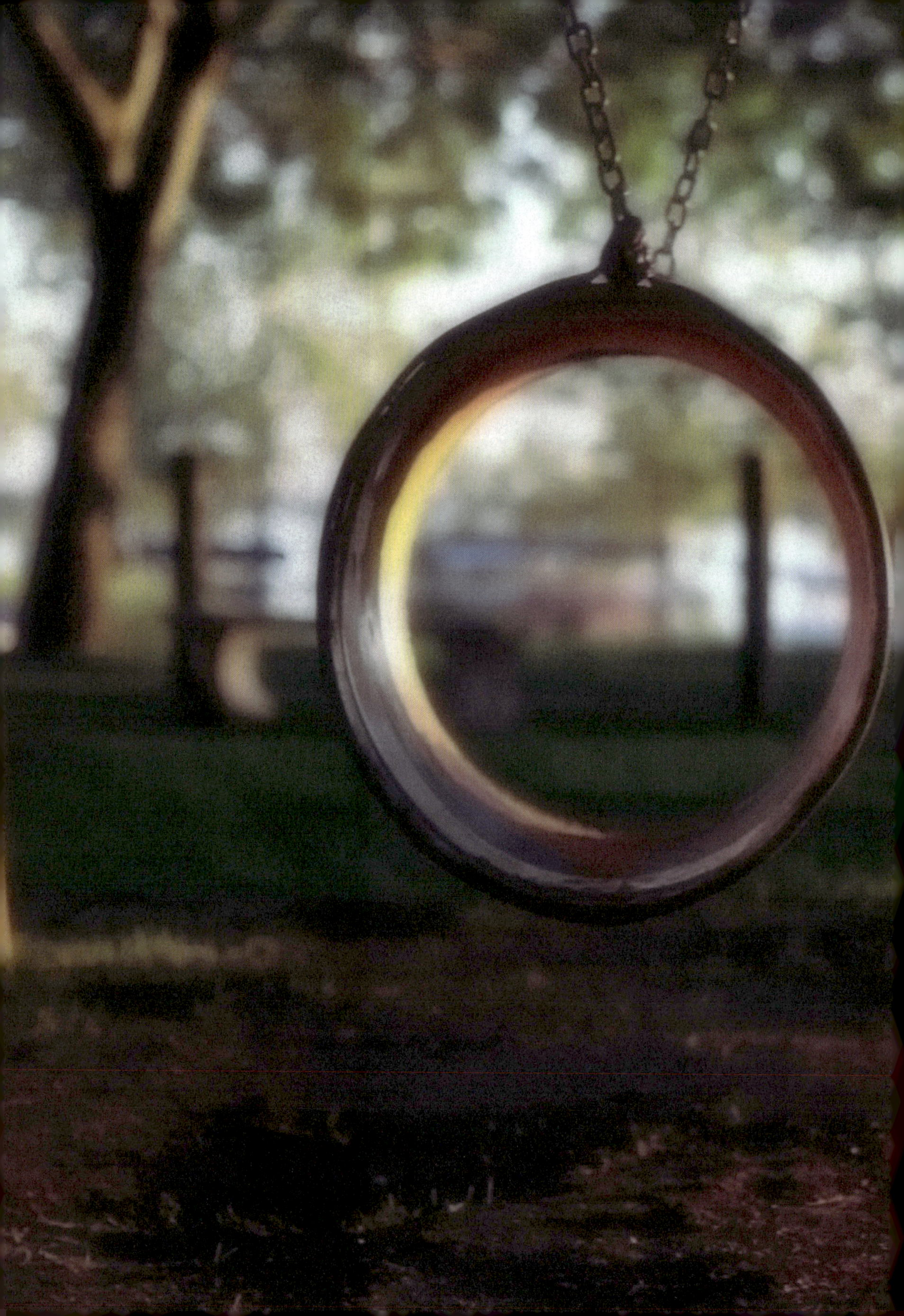

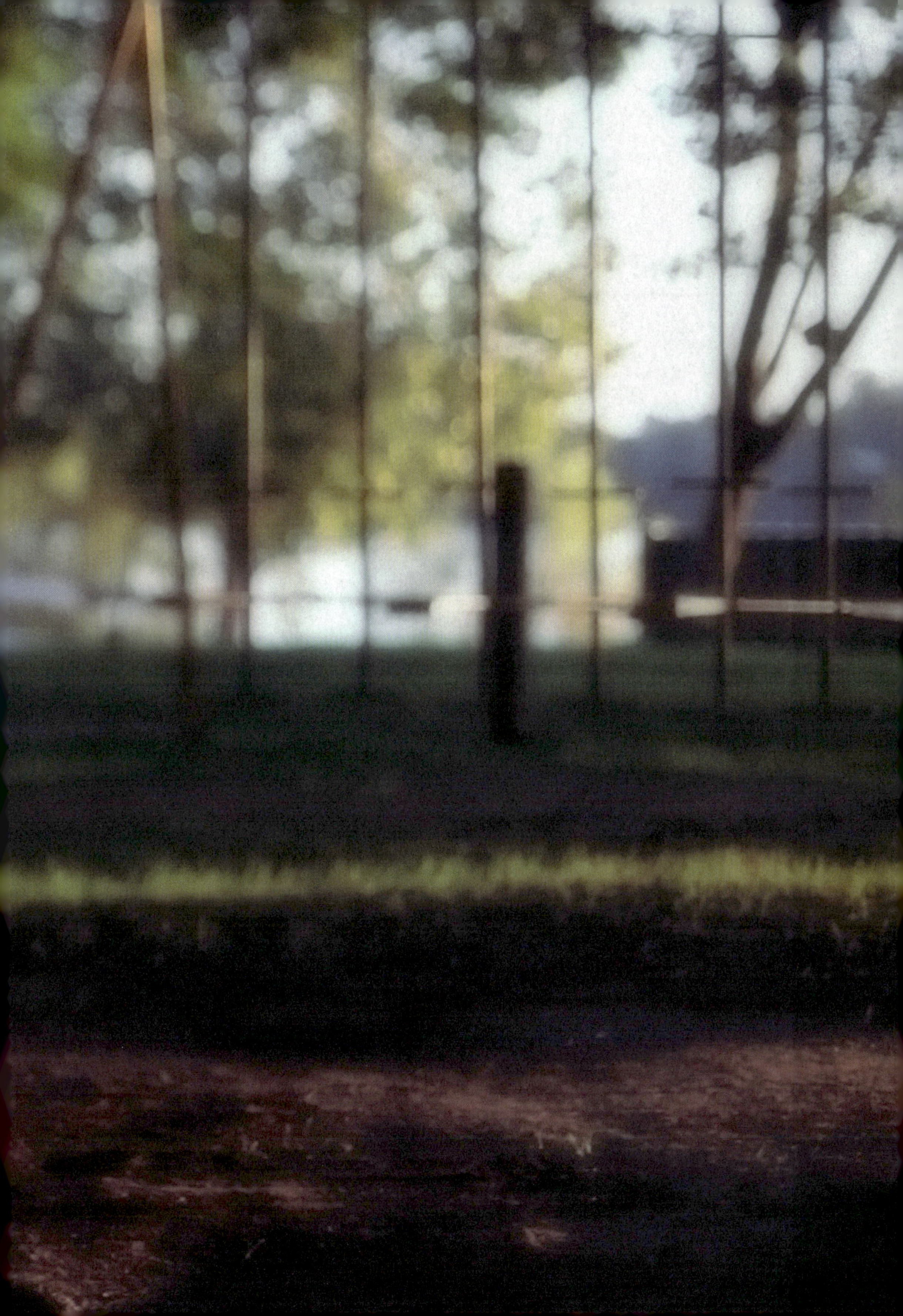

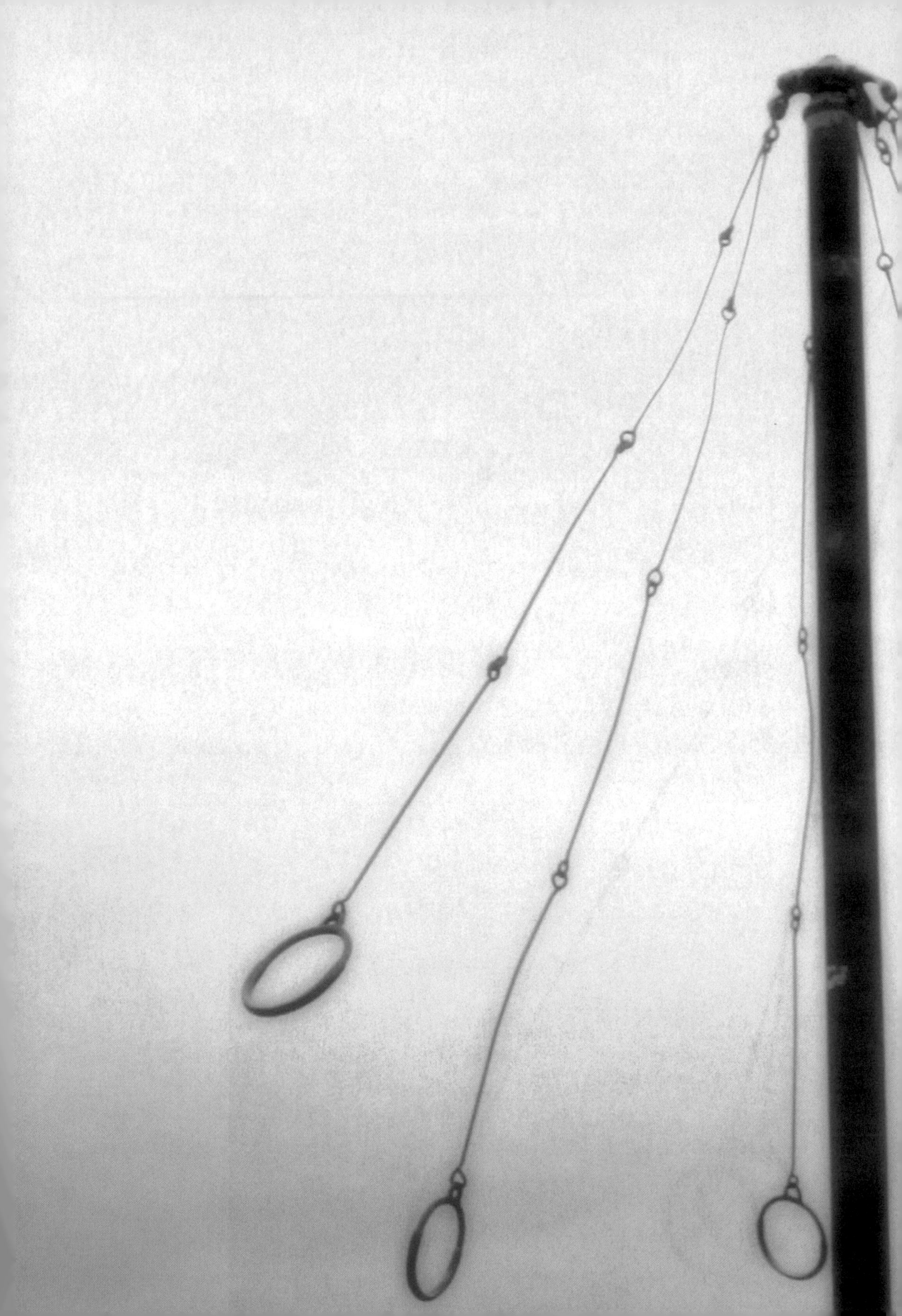

A ALMA DO OSSO (THE SOUL OF THE BONE)
2004

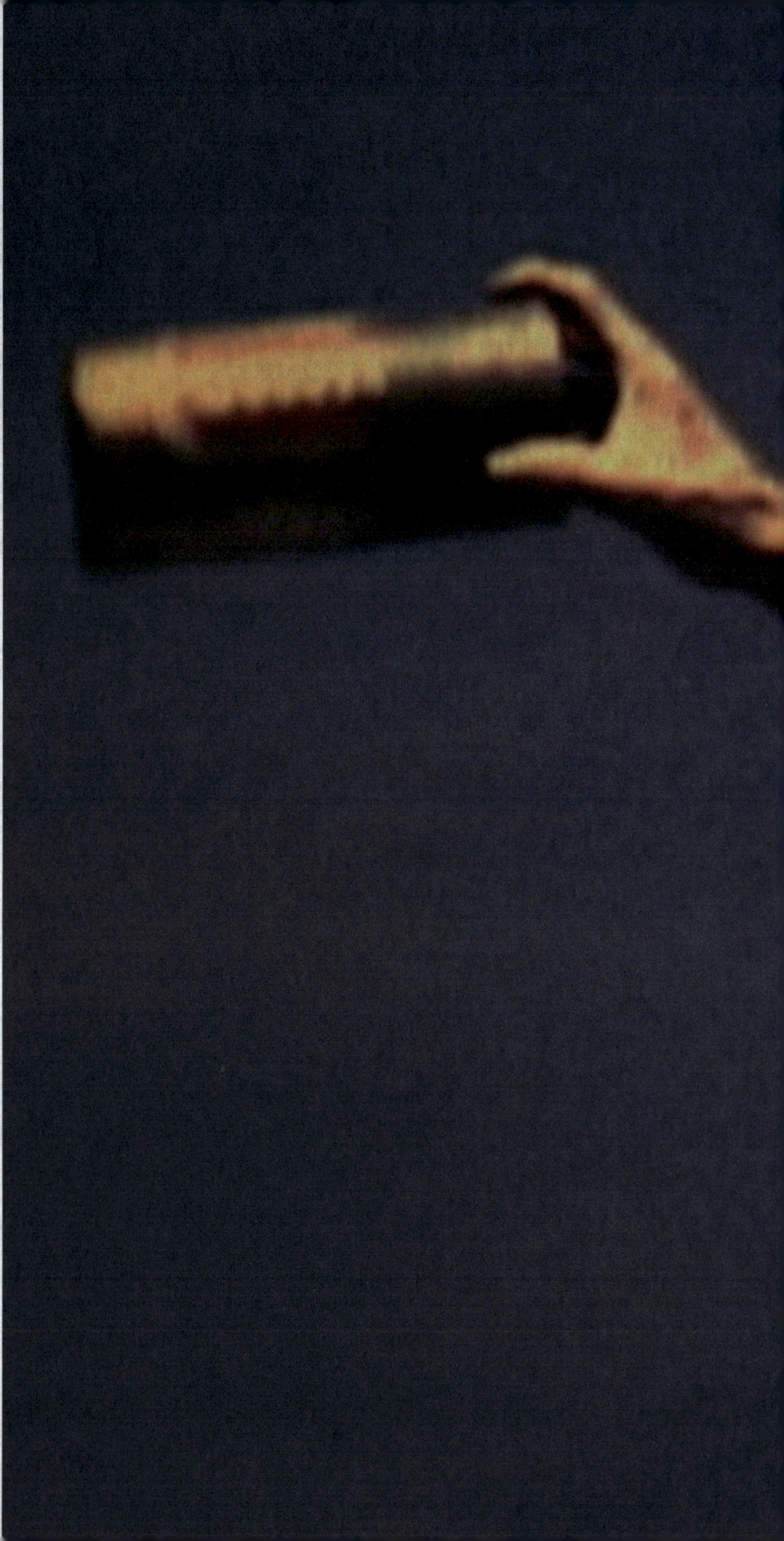

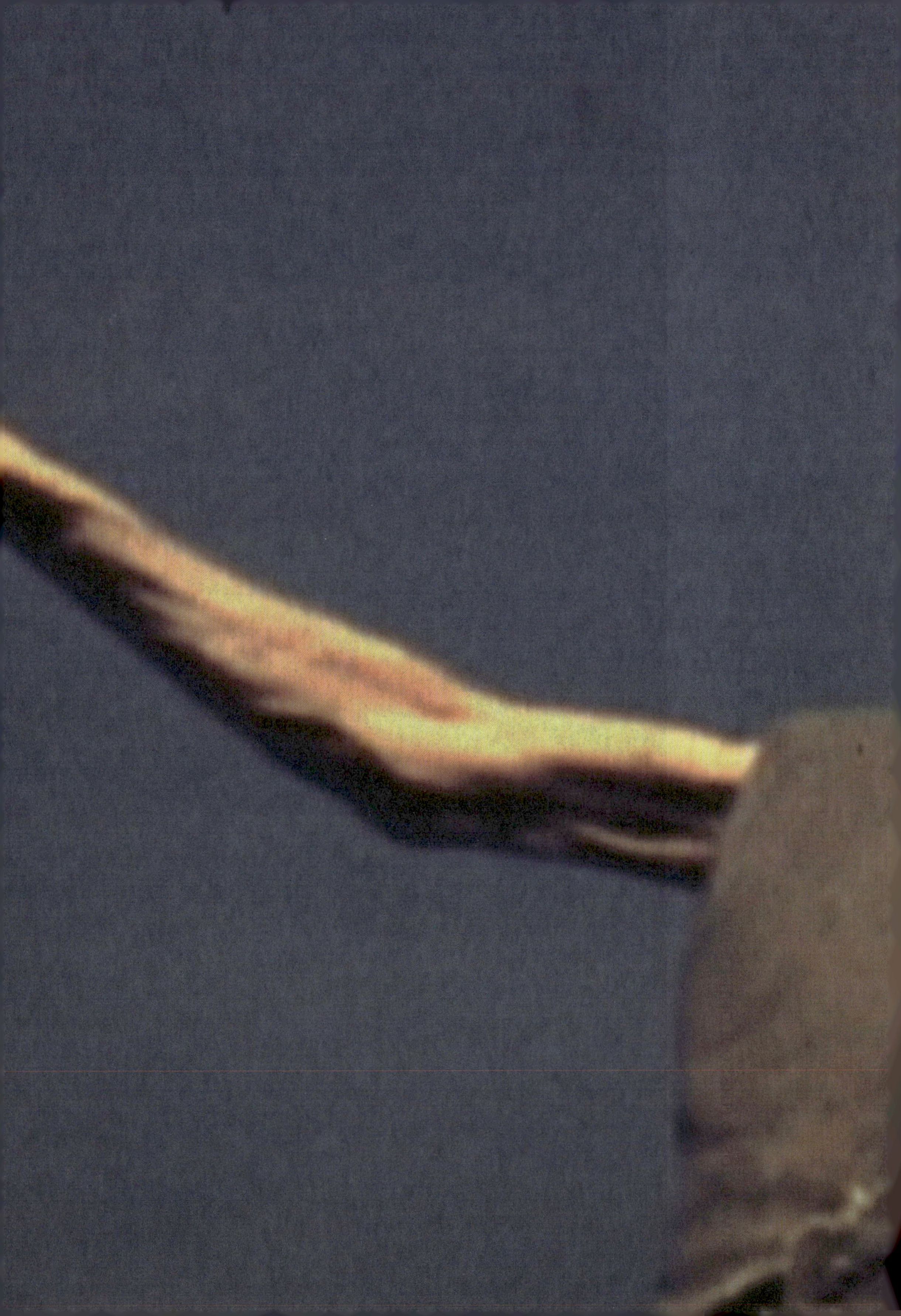

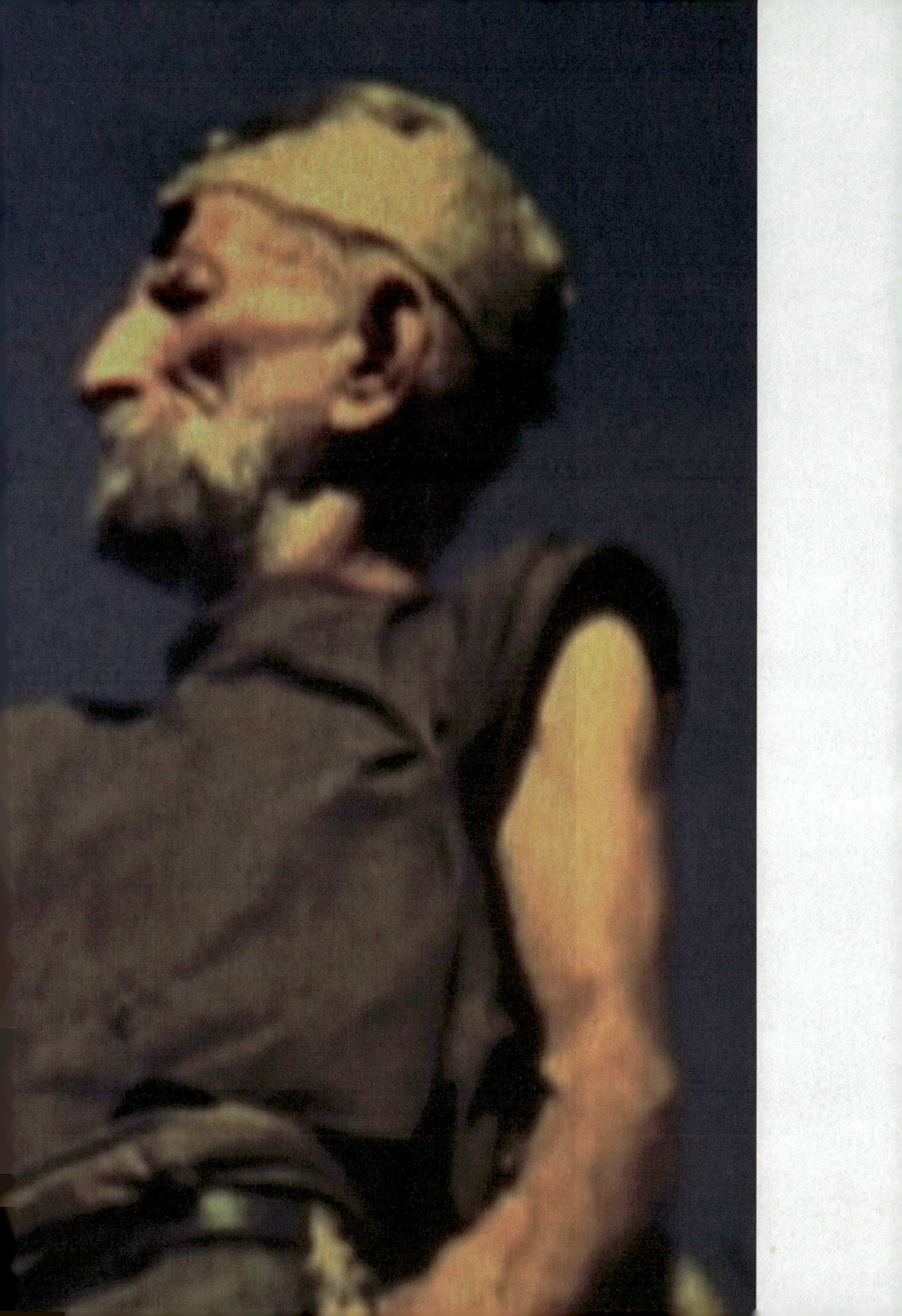

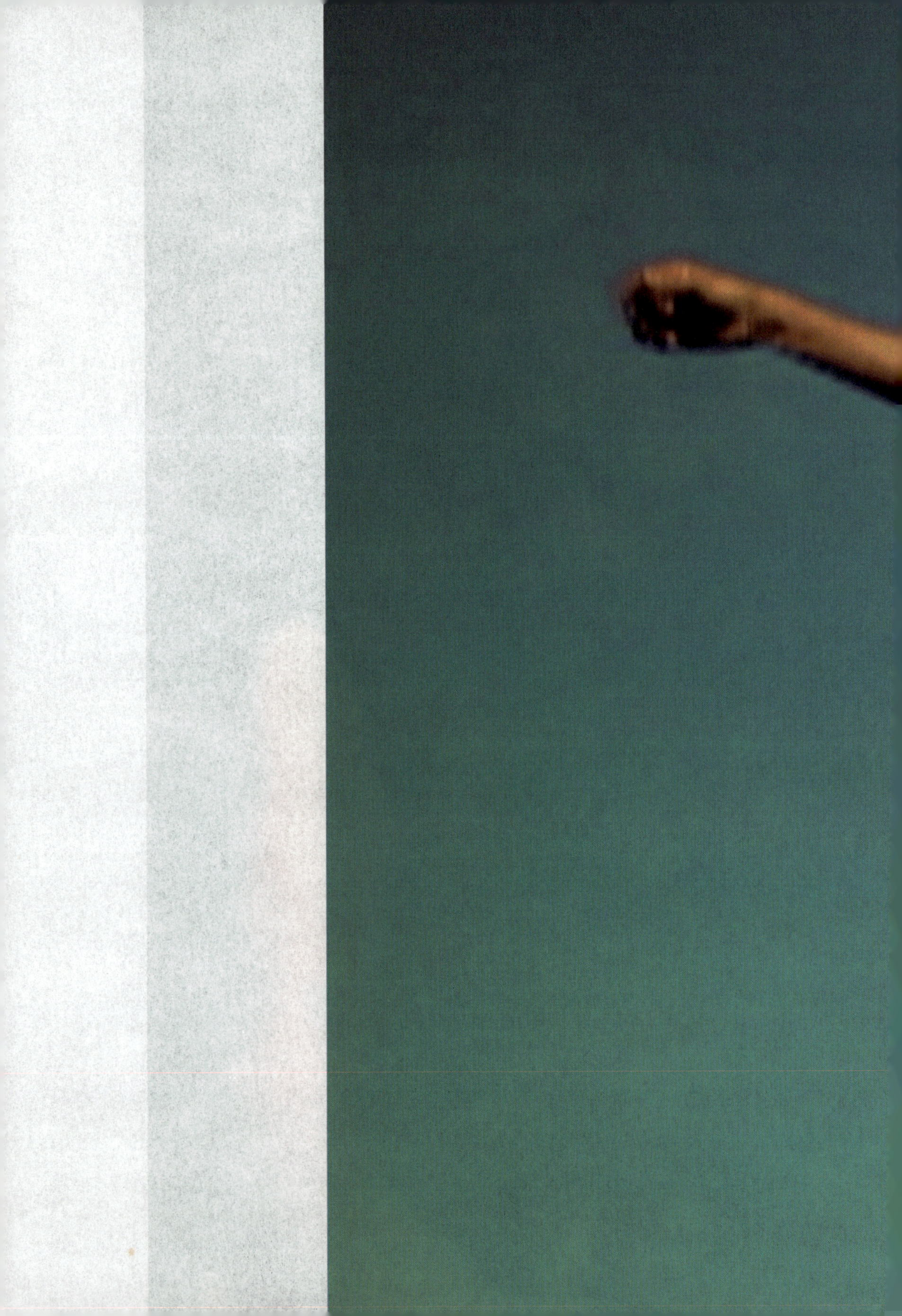

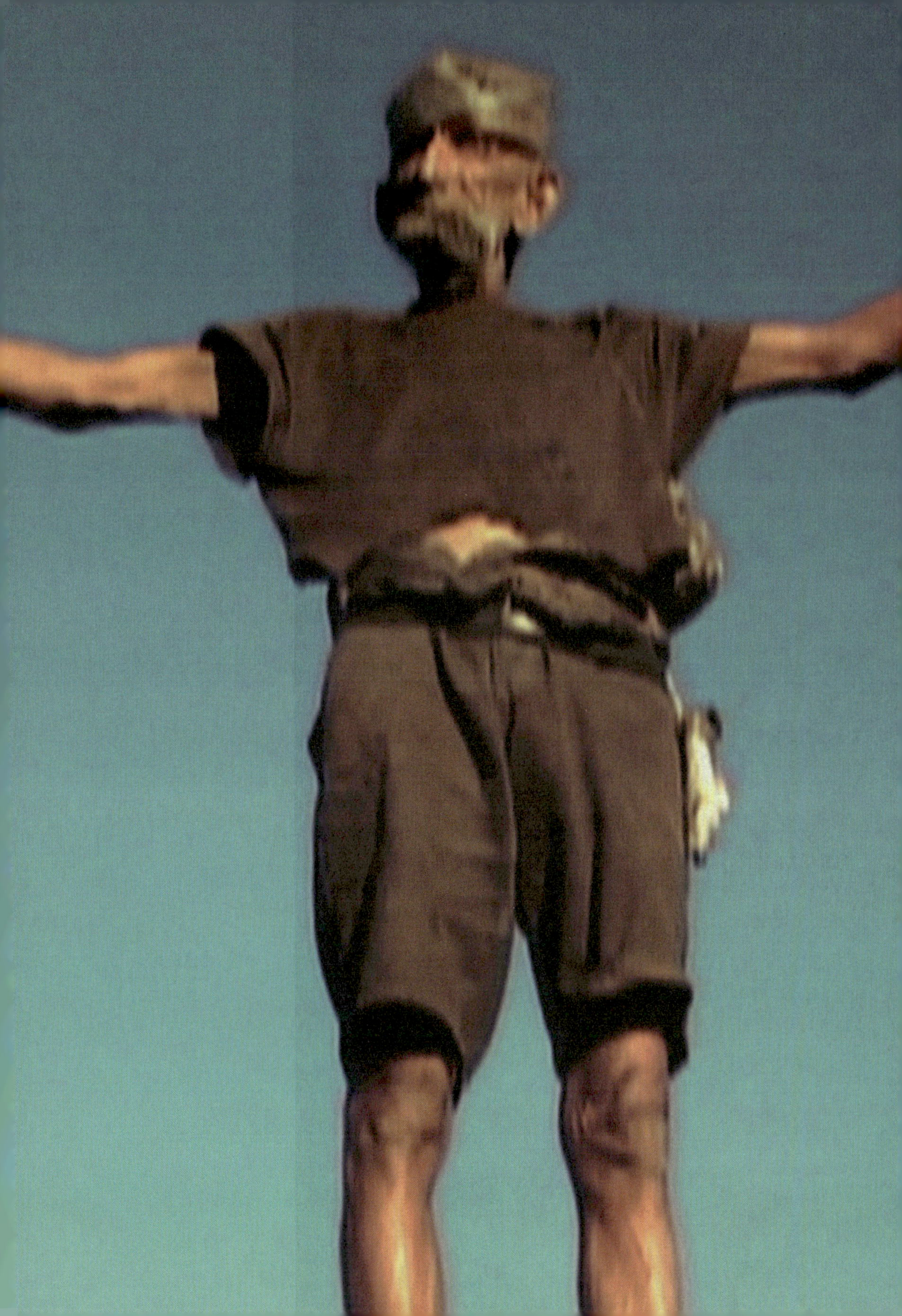

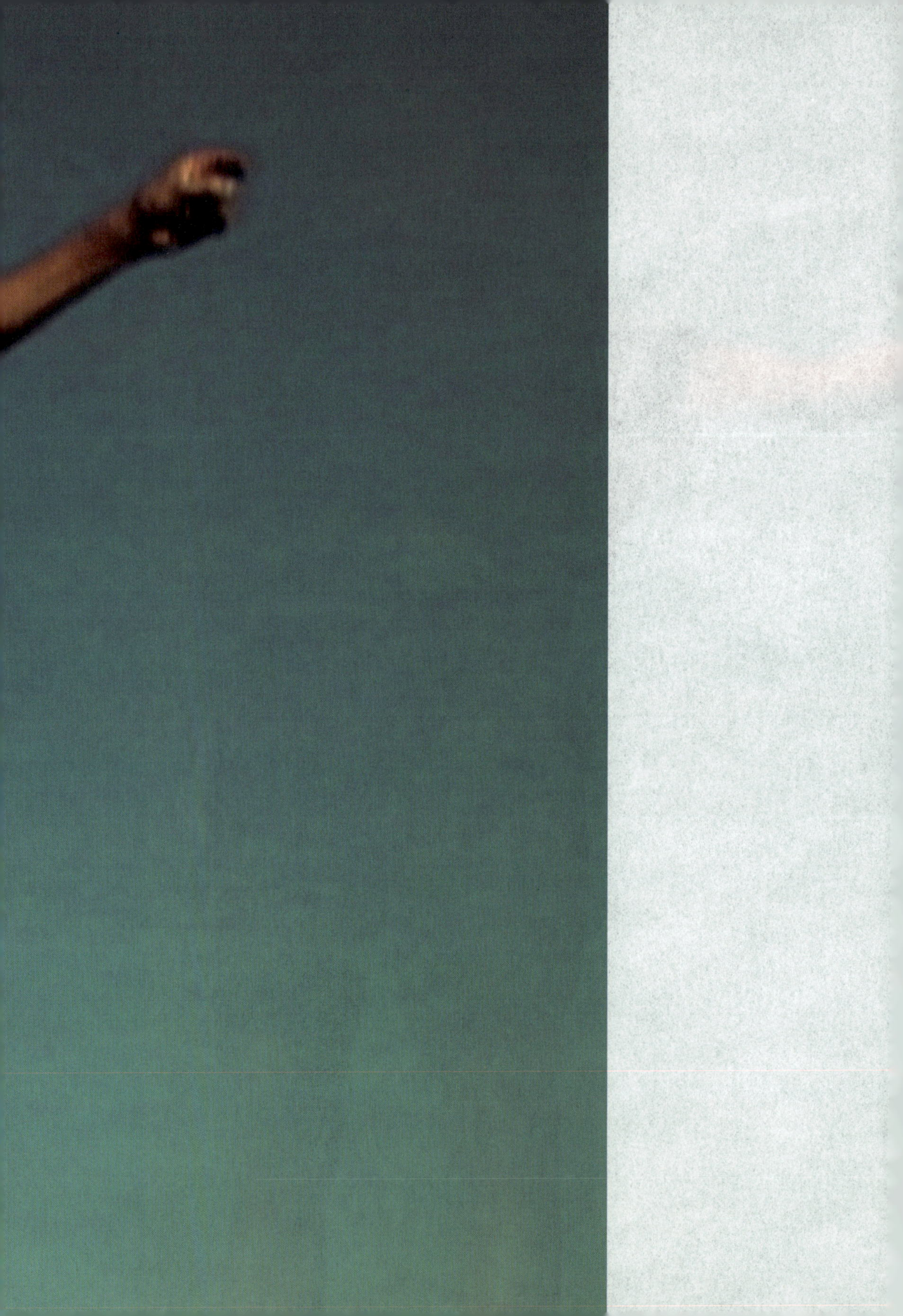

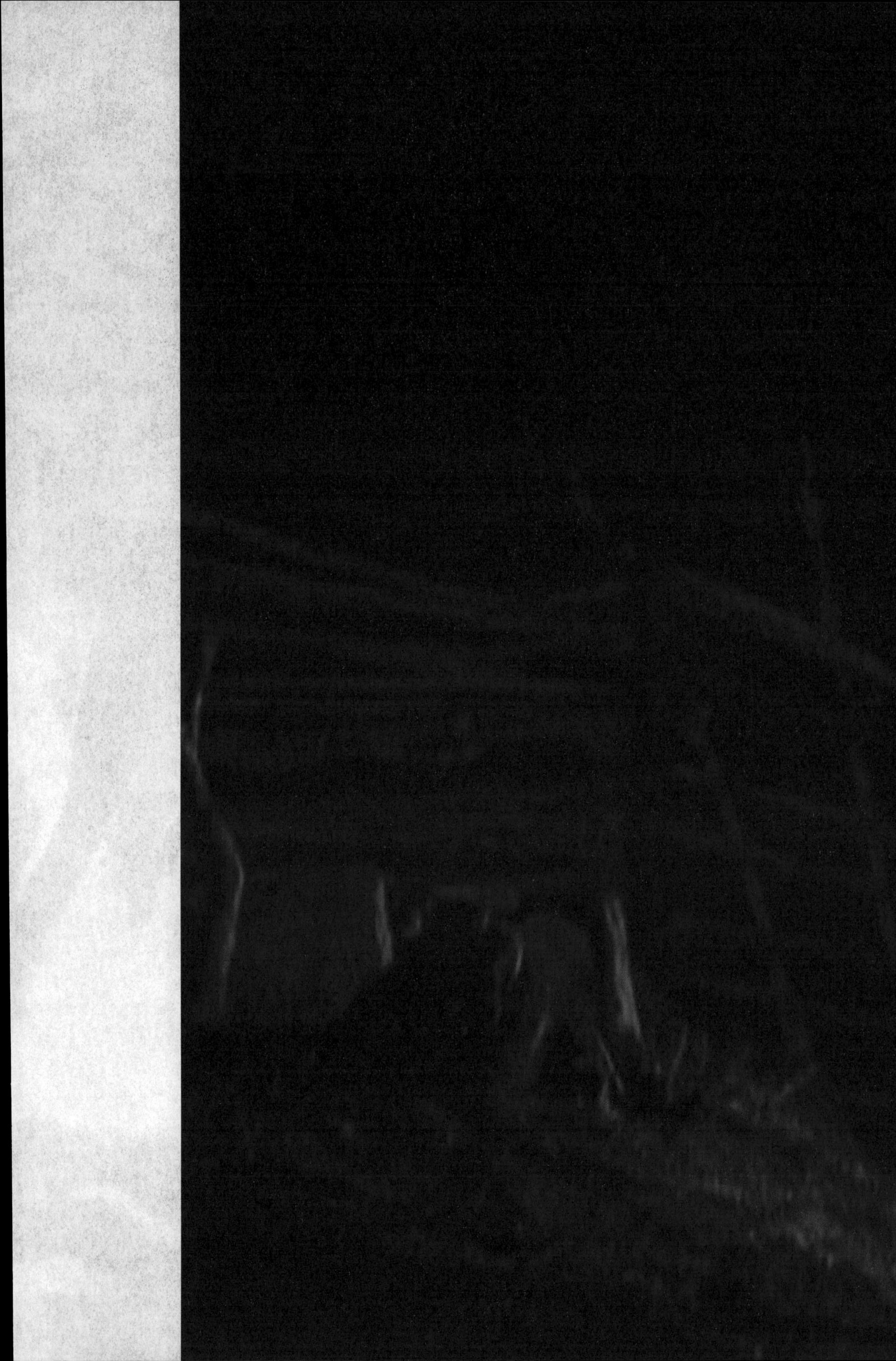

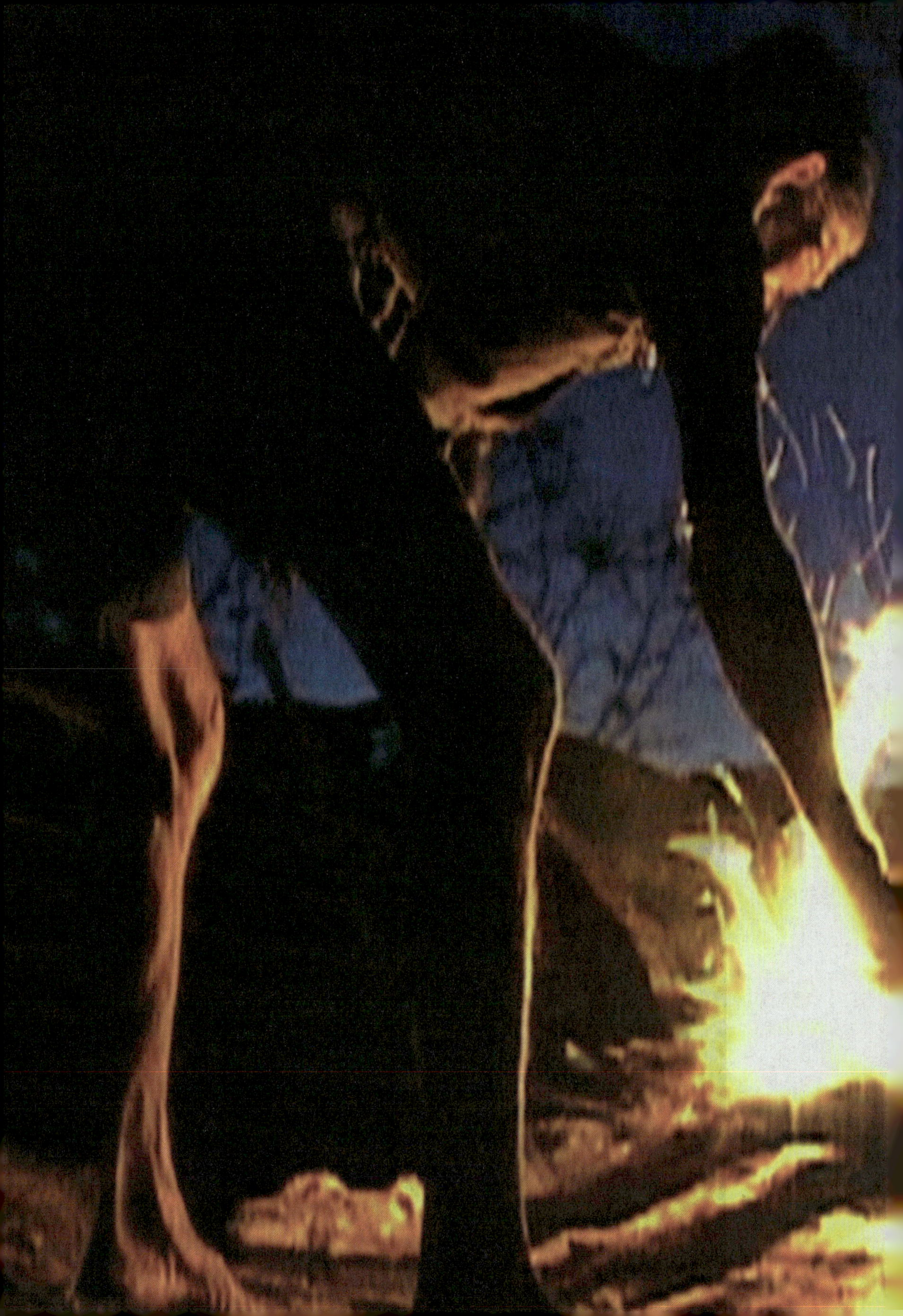

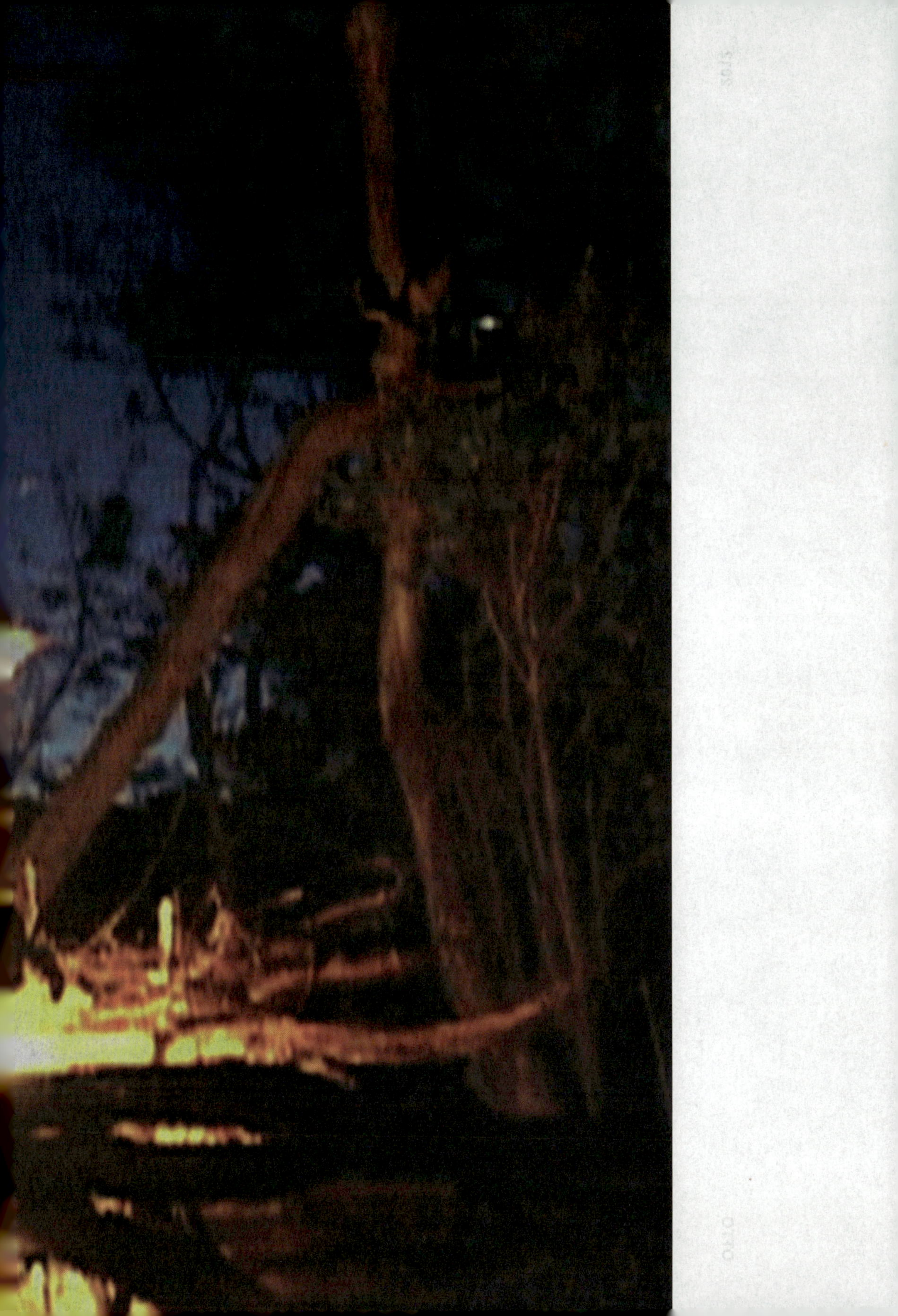

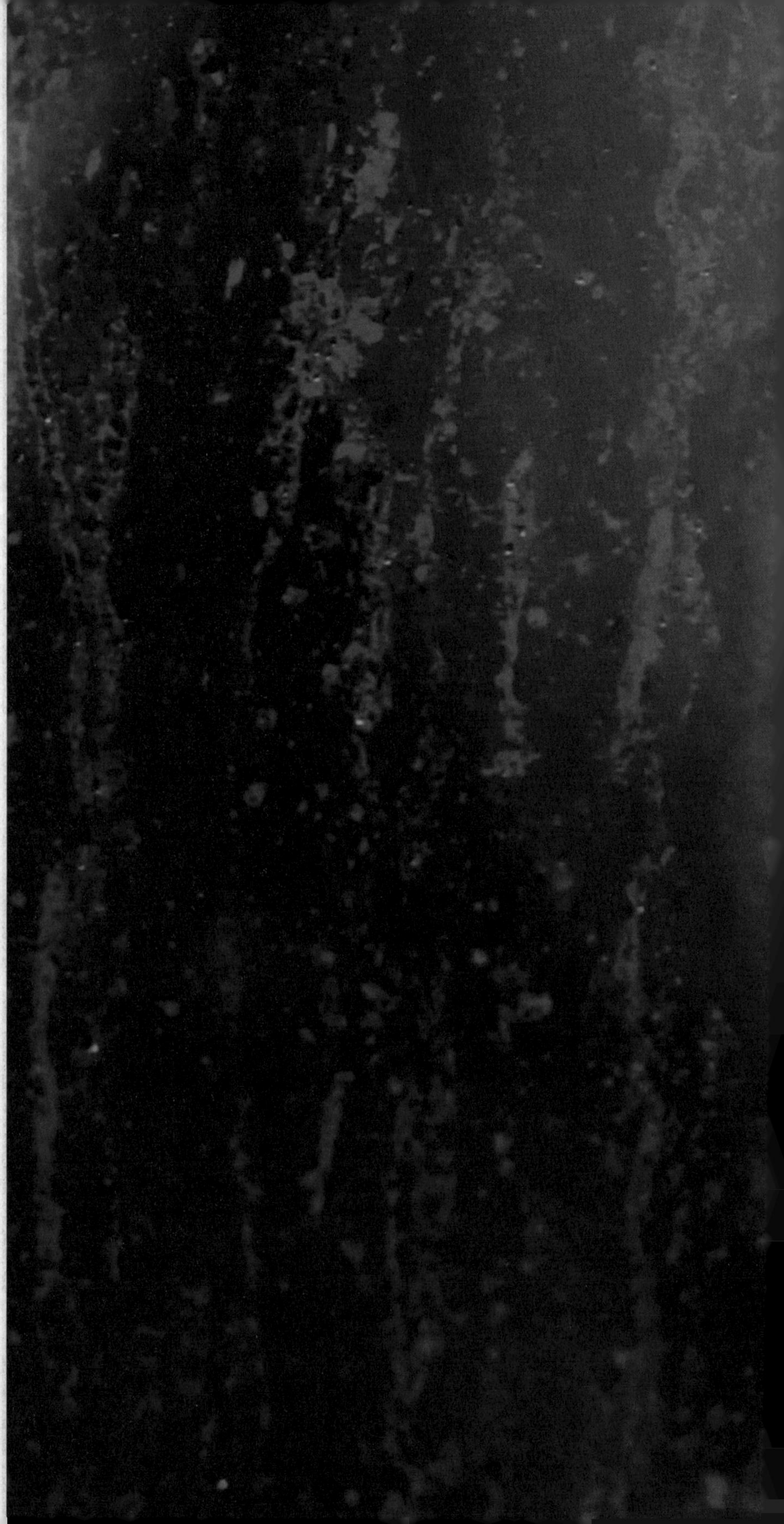

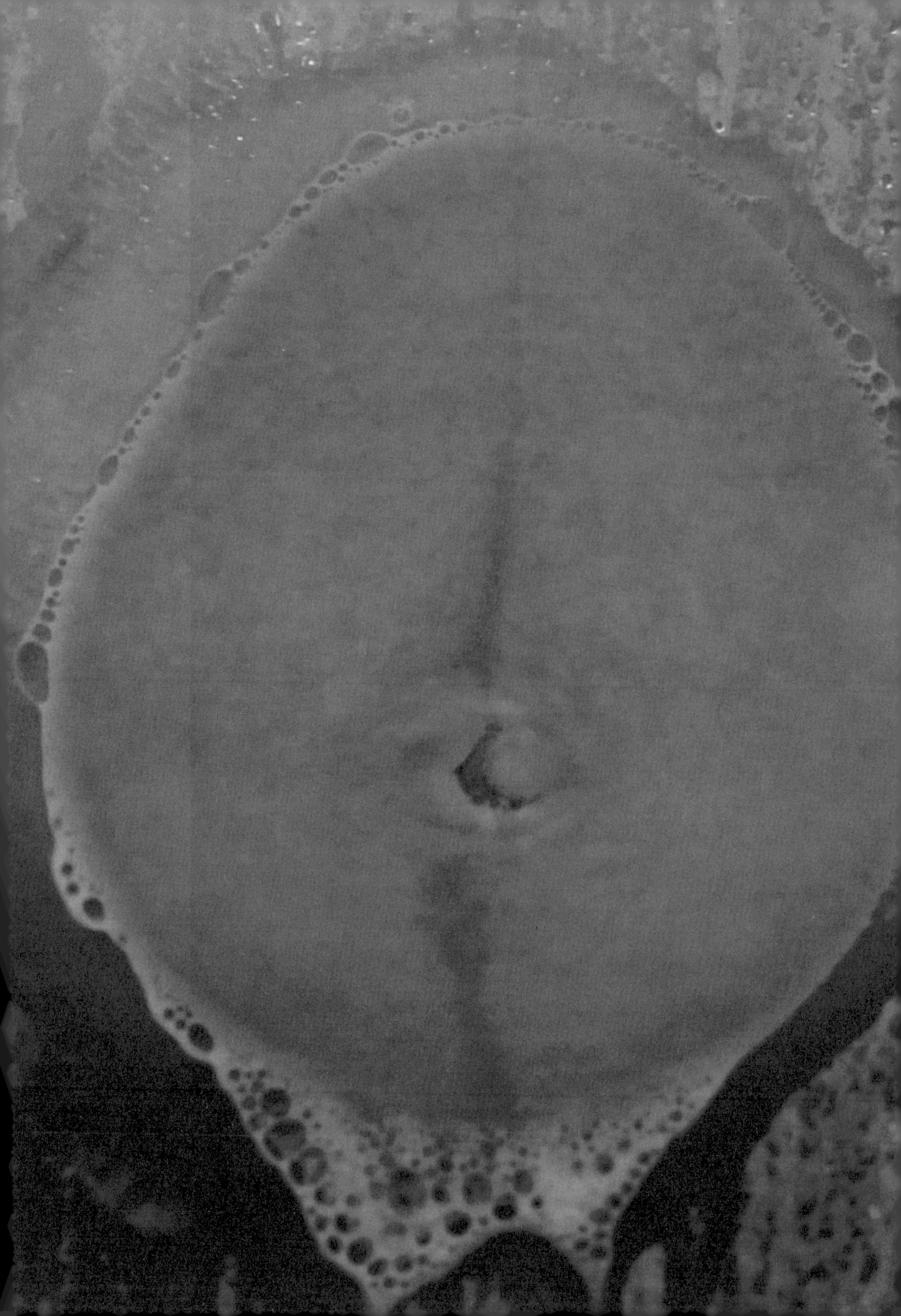